Distinguishing Characteristics of Gifted Students With Disabilities

Distinguishing Characteristics of Gifted Students With Disabilities

Terry Friedrichs, Ph.D.

PRUFROCK PRESS, INC.

ISBN 1–882664–69–8

Prufrock Press, Inc.
P.O. Box 8813
Waco, Texas 76714-8813
(800) 998-2208
Fax (800) 240-0333
http://www.prufrock.com

Table of Contents

Preface   xi

Introduction   1
- Themes in the Current Discussion on Gifted Students   1
  With Disabilities
- Our Current Lack of Knowledge on Distinguishing   3
  Traits: How it Hurts the Gifted Disabled
- Reasons for Learning More About the Identifying   4
  Characteristics of Gifted-Disabled Subpopulations
- A Literature-Based Search to Increase Knowledge   8
  About and Improve Identification of the Gifted
  Disabled   9
- Notes

1. Traits of Gifted Individuals With Mild Disabilities   13
- Learning   19
- Motivation   20
- Creativity   20
- Leadership/Social Development   20
- Additional Traits of the Gifted Learning Disabled   21
- Additional Traits of the Gifted Emotionally Disturbed   25
- Additional Traits of the Gifted Communication   27
  Disordered
- Notes   32

2. Traits of Gifted Physically Disabled Students   43
- Learning   43
- Motivation   44
- Creativity   44
- Leadership/Social Development   44
- Additional Traits of the Gifted Orthopedically Impaired   45
- Additional Traits of the Gifted Health Impaired   47
- Notes   50

3. Traits of Gifted Sensory-Impaired Students   53
- Learning   53
- Motivation   54
- Creativity   54
- Leadership/Social Development   54
- Additional Traits of the Gifted Visually Impaired   54
- Additional Traits of the Gifted Hearing Impaired   57
- Notes   60

4. Traits of Gifted Students With Multiple Disabilities   63
- Learning   63
- Motivation   65
- Creativity   65
- Leadership/Social Development   65
- Notes   66

5. Traits of Gifted Mentally Handicapped Students   67
- Learning   67
- Motivation   67
- Creativity   68
- An Update   68
- Notes   70

Conclusion   71
- Limitations on Use of Trait Descriptions   71
- Needs for Further Investigations on Traits   72
- Notes   73

References   74

Appendix   82

List of Tables

Table 1   Size of U.S. Gifted-Disabled Subpopulations
(Grades K–12)   6

Table 2   Eminent Persons With Disabilities   7

Table 3   Most Commonly Exhibited Traits   14
of Gifted-Disabled Subpopulations

Table 4   Additional Traits of the Gifted Learning Disabled   22

Table 5   Additional Traits of the Gifted   28
Emotionally Disturbed

Table 6   Additional Traits of the Gifted   30
Communication Disordered

Table 7   Additional Traits of the Gifted   46
Orthopedically Impaired

Table 8   Additional Traits of the Gifted Health Impaired   49

Table 9   Additional Traits of the Gifted Visually Impaired   56

Table 10   Additional Traits of the Gifted Hearing Impaired   59

Table 11   Additional Traits of the Gifted Multiply Disabled   64

Table 12   Additional Traits of the Gifted   68
Mentally Handicapped

●●●

To my parents

Bernadine and Eugene Friedrichs

and my grandparents

Michael J. McGrath   William L. Friedrichs
Alice McGrath Lee   Margaret Friedrichs

with appreciation and affection

●●●

Preface

This monograph is designed to inform a variety of audiences—parents, policy makers, teachers, and the public—about the traits of those increasingly touted but rarely identified students—gifted pupils with disabilities. In confirming the existence of the seemingly contradictory child who simultaneously has gifts and disabilities, this document may serve to confirm the judgment of many parents. Parents who correctly sense that their children are gifted, only to be flooded with depressing complaints about unsatisfactory school performance, should enjoy this document particularly. I hope that parents will become more knowledgeable and sensitive in their interactions with their gifted children with disabilities, and will be more effective advocates for gifted education assessments when they interact with professionals at their children's schools.

This book demonstrates gifted-disabled students are "on the fence"—they may or may not "make it." They are clearly shown to be a sizable population that has the potential to make it, given well-crafted identification policies meant to recognize strengths. I hope policy makers who read this document will be inspired to craft and implement such guidelines.

In graphically describing for the American public the complicated lives of the gifted pupils with disabilities, the public may begin to see the gifted disabled as a group that actually emerges victorious only after a protracted push-and-pull between specific strengths and weaknesses. This complex, realistic portrait may help members of the public, many of whom were weaned on television "movies of the week" in which high-potential persons with disabilities rise to world-class achievements in just two hours. This book should help readers begin to see and nurture the strengths of persons with disabilities whom they know—persons who may be gifted, but who continue to struggle.

Finally, I hope teachers who read this book will become more proficient at the school-based identification of these students. It is to these teachers that this monograph, drawn largely from studies of gifted-disabled children at school, is particularly directed.

Introduction

I mproving knowledge about the distinguishing traits of school-aged gifted students with disabilities is central to the current dialogue on how best to instruct these "twice-exceptional" pupils. It also is helpful to examine the ways in which a lack of knowledge about these characteristics may hurt gifted-disabled students and to analyze the many reasons that it is now essential to increase that knowledge.

Themes in the Current Discussion on Gifted Pupils With Disabilities

There are at least four themes running through current discussions about the twice-exceptional:
1. the scarcity of our core knowledge about gifted-disabled students' characteristics;
2. our ineffectiveness in finding students exhibiting these traits, using schools' traditional, standardized, and informal measures;
3. the importance of using alternative, informal means to identify these pupils; and
4. our lingering uncertainty over how to serve these students once they are identified.

A Dearth of Knowledge

Even researchers have little knowledge about the rich variety of traits shown by different twice-exceptional subpopulations,[1] traits that may be positive or negative characteristics, or positive ones masquerading as negative.[2] This lack of familiarity is due partly to an emphasis throughout the gifted education literature on high-achieving gifted children.[3]

This limited awareness is also related to a long-standing focus, dating back to the early 1970s, on the celebration, rather than the detailed scientific study, of the lives of gifted persons with disabilities. American culture tends to elevate to the status of icons a few twice-exceptional persons who rose to great prominence in the arts, politics, or business.[4] However, it does not explain in detailed fashion the qualities by which these persons reached those positions. The result of this cultural celebration has been to inspire readers, but not give them the facts that: (1) there are many gifted pupils with disabilities in today's schools,[5] and (2) there are contemporary lists of these pupils' traits that can be used to systematically find these students.[6] This monograph will address these two points.

On a hopeful note, since the early 1970s some descriptive works on gifted pupils with disabilities—professional books and articles containing varying levels of detail—have started to appear, including the 95 pieces covered in this document. This monograph, however, is the first in two decades to draw together works that cover a broad spectrum of twice-exceptional subpopulations.

The Failure of Traditional Identification

One consequence of the diffuse, and still relatively scanty, information on the gifted disabled has been an ongoing problem in identifying these pupils as gifted with sufficient frequency. Of the estimated 450,000 high-potential disabled pupils in America's K–12 public and private schools,[7] very few actually have been identified as gifted.[8]

Without an idea of what twice-exceptional pupils act like day-to-day, teachers nominating pupils for gifted education assessment must rely on those traditional identification measures used with the overall school population. Unfortunately, high-potential disabled students tend to score relatively low on group-administered, standardized achievement and intelligence tests, which still have a powerful impact on nominations for and admittance to gifted education programs.[9] The twice-exceptional may have perceptual, memory, attention, or experiential deficits, specific areas of difficulty that result in low scores—scores that, in turn, prevent these pupils from reaching school districts' total-test cut-off scores for gifted status.[10] These problems also obscure from referring educators the higher-level thinking skills that frequently equal those of gifted nondisabled peers.[11]

A Need for Alternative Identification

What identification processes will effectively assess the higher-level thinking skills and other strengths of high-potential students with disabilities? Trait checklists of these strengths have been endorsed as very appropriate instruments, and have been utilized effectively in schools.[12] Sadly, few such checklists exist, and those that do exist were often designed only to help identify generically defined "gifted-disabled" students.[13]

Here, identification checklists will be tailored to nine groups of twice-exceptional students, because the subgroups can be so different from each another.[14] Lists of the traits of each group of high-potential disabled students—and descriptions of how the compiled characteristics play themselves out in teachers' classrooms—also are provided to help educators identify these students.[15]

A Need for Alternative Programming

With their unusual clusters of traits and their need for unusual identification procedures, it is not surprising that gifted-disabled subpopulations require modified gifted education programming. Up to the present time, with the exception of some fairly well-publicized, self-contained programs for the gifted disabled,[16] educators wishing to accelerate or enrich subject matter for students in these groups appear relegated to "doing the best they can." These teachers, without certain knowledge of what these pupils' traits are and how they affect the educational process, must simply modify individual assignments for what they *guess* to be the students' individual strengths and weaknesses.[17]

An Emphasis on Building Knowledge

In this monograph, I will address the first theme in the current dialogue on gifted students with disabilities: building knowledge. By building knowledge, I hope that readers will become more aware of, and hopefully "pull for," the twice-exceptional persons in their midst.

I hope educators will nominate gifted-disabled students with more frequency for gifted education assessment, and that educational researchers will construct more-effective identification mechanisms to find twice-exceptional students. All educators can work toward inaugurating more appropriate programming for these students' unique school-related needs.

Our Current Lack of Knowledge on Distinguishing Traits: How it Hurts the Gifted Disabled

There have been few appropriate perceptions, and many stereotypical expectations, about both gifted and disabled students. These stereotypical expectations have had a powerful, negative influence on educators who work with pupils who are simultaneously gifted and disabled. These educators rarely refer high-potential pupils with disabilities during school-based gifted education assessment and identification processes. The absence of appropriately high expectations for high-potential disabled pupils has led, in part, to the sad failure to fulfill potential among many of these students.

Stereotypical Expectations and Their Influence

Educators, even those who specialize in the education of the disabled and the gifted, frequently seem to think that the disabled are poor at doing many things, and that the gifted are good at most everything, like the television character Doogie Howser.[18] These expectations represent "old" knowledge that must be unlearned before "new" knowledge is assimilated.

The old knowledge, unfortunately, is powerful and intransigent. It is, in large, part responsible for the lack of referrals of disabled students to gifted education services,[19] and the dearth of nominations of high-potential pupils for disability services.[20] A lack of accurate knowledge about the twice-exceptional certainly may have been responsible for special education teachers' failure to refer any of New York City's 60,000 disabled students for gifted services.[21]

Wasted Potential Stemming From Underidentification of Giftedness

One sad result of the failure of American schools to identify twice-exceptional students as gifted[22] is that disabled children's unrecognized gifts can wither away slowly. This was true of Jason, a third-grade youth whom I taught in a remedial reading setting. Jason was gifted in oral language and general information, but had poor grades in reading, spelling, writing, and social studies. Because of his school's constant attention to his deficits and absence of attention to his strengths, Jason began to believe that he lacked skill in *all* of the language arts and in his ability to acquire information. By junior high, he was earning Ds in all subjects.

Another possible outcome of underidentification is that widely acknowledged gifts may disappear quickly and sometimes dramatically. One high school student, particularly well-known for his leadership, felt his weaknesses magnified and his strengths grossly undervalued, and so committed suicide.[23]

Reasons for Learning More About the Identifying Characteristics of Gifted-Disabled Subpopulations

Beyond the fact that the twice-exceptional may be hurt by educators' lack of knowledge about them, why should educators and parents learn about these characteristics? There are at least three reasons:

1. the large number of gifted students with disabilities;
2. these pupils' potential noteworthiness; and
3. the currently strong push to better identify them.

Numbers

Table 1 provides estimates of the large number of students in the various groups of high-potential subpopulations with disabilities. These subpopulations are grouped in the categories and the order in which they will be discussed in this paper. (See Notes 1 and 2 on the derivation of these estimates.)

Noteworthiness of Gifted Individuals With Disabilities

As can be seen in Table 2, there are many especially prominent achievers among these groups. Notable contemporary members of various twice-exceptional groups include numerous young, gifted persons with disabilities, such as Dack Akselle, a 12-year-old Virginia boy in a wheelchair who competed in marathons.[24]

Current Drive to Improve Identification of Giftedness

Various groups, including parents, legislators, and educators of the gifted have displayed rising interest in reversing the underidentification of high-potential disabled students. In an era of increasing site-based and community-centered school management,[25] some parent groups have successfully advocated for gifted education services for their gifted children with disabilities.[26]

In addition, increasing Congressional support has been seen for gifted education. In 1987, supporters of the Jacob Javits Gifted and Talented Education Act (a piece of federal legislation promulgated throughout the 1980s) eventually outnumbered critics—critics like the political pundit who once said that providing high-potential students with special services was like "giving the tall kids stilts." Although Javits Act funding often found itself under scrutiny at the Congressional chopping block, the act managed to survive and be renewed several times after its passage, spawning much research and many innovative programming efforts discussed at national gifted education conventions. [27] It targeted much-needed federal resources for the identification and teaching of the gifted and, more specifically, the twice-exceptional.

Further, educators of the gifted have placed particular emphasis on gifted pupils with disabilities, as seen in state-level Department of Education publications[28] and in programs for conventions of statewide, national, and international organizations.[29] At the 1999 National

Table 1

Size of U.S. Gifted-Disabled Subpopulations (Grades K-12)

Gifted-Disabled Subgroup	Approximate Size of Gifted-Disabled Subgroup[1]	Approximate Size of Each Group With Disabilities (Gifted + Nongifted Together)[1]
Mildly Handicapped		
Learning Disabled	95,050	1,900,750
Emotionally Disturbed	17,100	342,300
Communication Disordered	55,700	1,114,400
Physically Disabled		
Orthopedically Impaired	2,350	46,700
Other Health Impaired	2,250	44,950
Sensory Impaired		
Visually Impaired	950	19,200
Hearing Impaired	2,250	45,050
Multiply Disabled	3,800	75,750
Mentally Handicapped	Uncertain[2]	577,750

[1] Ysseldyke and Algozzine (1992) report the 1990 size of each of the groups federally defined as "disabled" under the U.S. Education of All Handicapped Children Act. About 5% of each of these disabled groups would be presumed to be gifted, since there are about as many gifted persons among the handicapped as among the general population (Davis & Rimm, 1985), and approximately 5% of the general population currently is identified as "gifted" in public schools (Ysseldyke & Algozzine, 1992). Thus, for Table 1, the size of each gifted-disabled subpopulation was calculated by taking 5% of each of Ysseldyke and Algozzine's estimates for each overall "disabled" population.

[2] The number of gifted mentally handicapped persons is probably far less than 5% of 577,750. This is because mentally handicapped persons generally lack enough of the intellectual capacity that is so important in producing creative, achievement, and leadership giftedness. The *exact* number of gifted mentally handicapped persons currently is unknown, however. This is because, to the present time, no scholar in the education of the disabled or the gifted has provided a widely read formula for precisely calculating the number of these students.

Table 2

Eminent Persons With Disabilities

Learning Disabled	Emotionally Disturbed	Communication Disordered	Ortho-pedically Impaired	Health Impaired	Visually Impaired	Hearing Impaired	Multi-handicapped
Hans Christian Andersen	Thomas Hardy	Henry Luce	Edgar Cayce	Rachel Carson	Louis Braille	Ludwig von Beethoven	Thomas Edison
Albert Einstein	Victor Hugo	Jack Paar	Marlene Dietrich	Marlene Dietrich	Ray Charles	Alexander Graham Bell	Antonio Gramsci
George Patton	Julius Huxley	Lewis Carroll	Uri Geller	T.S. Eliot	Joseph Pulitzer	Louis Sullivan	Charles Steinmetz
Woodrow Wilson	John Greenleaf Whittier		Peter Hurkos	Thor Hyerdahl	Stevie Wonder		
W.B. Yeats	Yukio Mishima		Carl Jung	Flannery O'Connor			
			Louis Leakey	Pope Paul VI			
				Jessamyn West			
				Andrew Wyeth			
(Aaron, Phillips, & Larsen, 1988; Patten, 1972; Thompson, 1971)	(Goertzel, Goertzel, & Goertzel, 1978; Maker, 1977)	(Davis & Rimm, 1985; McGreevey, 1992)	(Goertzel et al., 1978; Karnes, Shwedel, & Lewis, 1983)	(Goertzel et al., 1978)	(Baker, 1972; Maker & Grossi, 1985)	(Karnes et al., 1983; Sarnecky & Michaud, 1979)	(Goertzel et al., 1978; Maker, 1977)

Association for Gifted Children (NAGC) convention, many of the sessions dealt with twice-exceptional students.[30]

A Literature–Based Search to Increase Knowledge About and Improve Identification of the Gifted Disabled

The appendix lists the 26 journals and four books that were considered in the development of this book (see Appendix, "Sources Consulted"). The relevant articles and books on characteristics of the twice-exceptional encompass case studies, expert opinions, clinical judgments, correlational research, and experimental inquiries and describe observable traits that might be displayed by members of each group of gifted-disabled learners. For each of the nine twice-exceptional groups, lists of distinctive traits were grouped into four familiar trait categories of learning, motivation, creativity, and leadership.[31] Further, to ease and illuminate discussion, trait similarities were noted within five groups: gifted mildly handicapped, physically impaired, sensory impaired, multiply disabled, and mentally handicapped students.

Notes

1. Whitmore, J. R., & Maker, C. J. (1985). *Intellectual giftedness in disabled persons*. Rockville, MD: Aspen.
2. Friedrichs, T. P. (1990). *Gifted handicapped students: The way forward*. Richmond, VA: Virginia Department of Education.
3. Davis, G. A., & Rimm, S. B. (1985). *Education of the gifted and talented*. Englewood Cliffs, NY: Prentice-Hall;
   VanTassel-Baska, J. (1991). Serving the disabled gifted through educational collaboration. *Journal for the Education of the Gifted, 14*, 246–266.
4. Baker, H. J. (1970). *Biographical sagas of willpower*. New York: Vantage Press;
   Patten, M. B. (1972). Visually mediated thinking: A report on the case of Albert Einstein. *Journal of Learning Disabilities, 6*, 415–420;
   Thompson, L. J. (1971). Language disabilities in men of eminence. *Journal of Learning Disabilities, 4*, 39–50.
5. Davis & Rimm, 1985;
   Nielsen, M. E., Higgins, L. D., Hammond, A. E., & Williams, R. A. (1993, September/October). Gifted children with disabilities. *Gifted Child Today, 16*(5), 9–12.
6. Baum, S. (1988). An enrichment program for gifted learning disabled students. *Gifted Child Quarterly, 32*, 226–230;
   Johnsen, S. K., & Corn, A. L. (1989). The past, present, and future of education for gifted children with sensory and/or physical disabilities. *Roeper Review, 12*, 13–23;
   Miller, L. K. (1989). *Musical savants: Exceptional skill in the mentally retarded*. Hillsdale, NJ: Lawrence Erlbaum;
   Whitmore, J. R. (1980). *Giftedness, conflict, and underachievement*. Boston: Allyn and Bacon.
7. Davis & Rimm, 1985.
8. Nielsen et al., 1993;
   Porter, R. M. (1982). The gifted handicapped: A status report. *Roeper Review, 4*, 24–25;
   Whitmore & Maker, 1985.
9. Baum, S., & Owen, S. V. (1988). High ability/learning disabled students: How are they different? *Gifted Child Quarterly, 32*, 311–316;
   Fox, L. H. (1981). Identification of the academically gifted. *American Psychologist, 36*, 1103–1111;
   Harrington, R. G. (1982). Caution: Standardized testing may be hazardous to the health of intellectually gifted children. *Education, 103*, 112–117;
   Rawson, M. (1968). *Developmental language disability: Adult accomplishments of dyslexic boys*. Baltimore: Johns Hopkins Press;

Schiff, M. M., Kaufman, A. S., & Kaufman, N. L. (1981). Scatter analysis of WISC-R profiles for learning disabled children with superior intelligence. *Journal of Learning Disabilities, 14*, 400–404.

10. Fox, L. H., Brody, L., & Tobin, D. (1983). *Learning-disabled/gifted children: Identification and programming.* Baltimore: University Park Press; Johnsen & Corn, 1989; Whitmore & Maker, 1985.

11. Fox et al., 1983; Whitmore & Maker, 1985.

12. Udall, A. J., & Maker, C. J. (1983). A pilot program for elementary-age learning-disabled gifted students. In L. H. Fox, L. Brody, & D. Tobin (Eds.), *Learning-disabled/gifted children: Identification and programming* (pp. 223–242). Baltimore: University Park Press; Whitmore & Maker, 1985.

13. Whitmore & Maker, 1985.

14. Whitmore & Maker, 1985.

15. Whitmore & Maker, 1985.

16. Baldwin, L. J., & Garguilo, D. A. (1983). A model program for elementary age learning-disabled/gifted children. In L. H. Fox, L. Brody, & D. Tobin (Eds.), *Learning-disabled/gifted children: Identification and programming* (pp. 207–222). Baltimore: University Park Press; Barton, J. E., & Starnes, W. T. (1989). Identifying distinguishing characteristics of gifted and talented/learning disabled students. *Roeper Review, 12*, 23–29; Nielsen et al., 1993; Udall & Maker, 1983.

17. Daniels, P. (1983). Teaching the learning-disabled/gifted child. In L. W. Fox, L. Brody, & D. Tobin (Eds.), *Learning-disabled/gifted children: Identification and programming* (pp. 37–49). Baltimore: University Park Press.

18. Whitmore & Maker, 1985.

19. Whitmore & Maker, 1985.

20. Senf, G. M. (1983). The nature and identification of learning disabilities and their relationship to the gifted child. In L. H. Fox, L. Brody, & D. Tobin (Eds.), *Learning disabled/gifted children: Identification and programming.* Baltimore: University Park Press.

21. Davis & Rimm, 1985; Eisenberg, D., & Epstein, E. (1981, December). *The discovery and development of giftedness in handicapped children.* Paper presented at the CEC-TAG Topical Conference on the Gifted and Talented Child, Orlando, FL.

22. Davis & Rimm, 1985; Eisenberg & Epstein, 1981; Osborne, J. K., & Byrnes, D. A. (1990, May/June). Gifted, disaffected, disruptive youth and the alternative school. *Gifted Child Today, 13*(3), 45–48;

Porter, 1982;
Whitmore & Maker, 1985.
23. Delisle, J. (1988, January/February). Striking out: Suicide and the gifted adolescent. *Gifted Child Today, 11*(1), 41–44.
24. Hallahan, D. P., & Kauffman, J. M. (1986). *Introduction to special education* (3rd ed.). Englewood Cliffs, NJ: Prentice-Hall.
25. Chubb, J. E., & Moe, T. M. (1990). *Politics, markets, and America's schools.* Washington, DC: Brookings Institution;
Odden, A., & Clune, W. (1995). Improving educational productivity and finance. *Educational Researcher, 24*(9), 6–10.
26. Barton & Starnes, 1989.
27. National Association for Gifted Children (NAGC). (1995). *Annual national convention program.* Washington, DC: Author.
28. Friedrichs, 1990.
29. National Association for Gifted Children (NAGC). (1999). *Annual national convention program.* Washington, DC: Author;
Savage, L., & Woodrum, D. (1988, May 6). *Presentation on identification of gifted LD students using Renzulli-Hartman Scales.* West Virginia TAG-GLD Conference, South Charleston.
30. NAGC, 1999.
31. Renzulli, J. S., Hartman, R. K., & Callahan, C. M. (1971). Teacher identification of superior students. *Exceptional Children, 38,* 211–214.

Traits of Gifted Students With Mild Disabilities

Despite the severity and pervasiveness of their school-related difficulties, learning-disabled (LD), emotionally disturbed (ED), and
communication-disordered students are considered "mildly" disabled, presumably because their learning and emotional problems are
less severe than those of other disabled youth.[1] Whether or not these difficulties are severe during the school years, these troubles frequently go
undetected before school entrance. In fact, parents of some high-potential youth with mild impairments are often surprised when school officials diagnose disabilities in their children for the first time.[2]

On the other hand, like parents of many preschool gifted youth,
they may be well-positioned to see the positive traits overlooked by the
teachers of their school-aged children.[3] Educators may be puzzled by the
ups and downs between and within these pupils' performance profiles
in the categories of learning, motivational, creativity, and leadership
skills.[4] To increase sensitivity toward these pupils and to improve the
accuracy of gifted education identification, teachers need specific information from parents and teacher-educators about these performance
inconsistencies.[5]

In describing gifted handicapped students, teacher-educators need
to respond particularly to regular-classroom educators for several reasons:
1. Most of these pupils spend the majority of their time in the regular
   classroom.[6]
2. There has been a national policy pressure for these students, like
   disabled pupils as a group, to spend most of their time in the regular classroom.[7]
3. There similarly have been rising expectations for classroom teachers
   to produce academic gains with these and other handicapped students.[8]

Table 3

Most Commonly Exhibited Traits of Gifted–Disabled Subpopulations

Learning	Mild			Physical		Sensory		Mult	Ment
	GLD	GED	GCD	GOI	GHthI	GVI	GHrI	GMltH	GMntH
1. Fund of Knowledge [GGG;McG; Msh; NHHW;SL;TB;WM;WMK]	+	+	+	+	+			—	—
2. Factual recall [Jhn86; M82; McG; Msh; NK; WM; WMK]	+	+	+	+		+			—
3. Auditory memory [FN; GGR; Jhn86; K54; 55; McG; MS; Msh; M82; WMK; WS]	—		—			+	—		—
4. Visual memory [BW; FMP; FN; GGG; K54; 55; MS; Mt; NK; WM; Wms]	—		+	+	+	—	+		—
5. Understanding of abstractions [FN; GGG; Jhn86; McG; Msh;NK; WAW; WM; WS]	+		+	+	+	+	+		—
6. Analytical thinking [FMP; FN; GGG; LD; M82; McG; NHHW; NK; Stv; RS; WM; WS]	+	—	+	+	+	—	+		—

#	Item	1	2	3	4	5	6	7	8
7.	Understanding of language concepts [DB; EI; FMP; GGG; K54; 55; M81; Msh; NHHW; RB; T; VY; WS; WM]	|	|	|	|	+		+	+
8.	Vocabulary [DB; FN; GGG; Jhn86; M82; McG; MS; Ptr; TB; VY; WM]				+	+	+	+	+
9.	Reading competence or enjoyment [APL; Fg; GGG; GTP; M82; McG; MS; Msh; Mt; Wms; W81]	|		+	+	+	+	+	+
10.	Average or above average grades overall [Ab; CP; DB; EI; Jhn86; Jns; Ldg; McG; NK; Snf; WM]	|		+	+		+	+	+
11.	Academic consistency [CP; Fg; GGG; Ksh; Jhn86; Jns; McG; Ptr; WAW]		|	+	+	|	|	+	+
12.	Quick closing of learning gaps [GGG; Ldg; WM]	|	|	+	+	+	+		

Motivation

#	Item	1	2	3	4	5	6	7	8
13.	Persistence on usual tasks [BLW; DB; EI; Fg; FN; GGG; Hlw; Jhn86; Mhy; MS; NHHW; TB]				|		|	|	|
14.	Frustration over academic tasks [B; BO; EI; F; FN; JB; Jsk; LD; M82; MS; Msh; Mt; NHHW; WM; WMW; Wms]	+	+	+	+		+	+	+

Table 3 continued

Most Commonly Exhibited Traits of Gifted–Disabled Subpopulations

	Mild			Physical		Sensory		Mult	Ment
	GLD	GED	GCD	GOI	GHthI	GVI	GHrI	GMltH	GMntH
Motivation continued									
15. Desiring learning challenge [GGG; GGR; Hlw; JB; McG; NHHW; WM]	+	+	+	+	+	+	+	+	+
16. Persistence in strengths, interests [Bm; BO; FBT; FMP; FN; GGG; GGR; Hlw; Jns; Jsk; M82; McG; Mhy; MS; Msh; NK; Ptr; R; U]	+	+	+	+	+	+	+	+	+
Creativity									
17. Problem solving [CI; Dls90; FMP; GGG; Jhn86; McG; NHHW; WAW; WM]	+	—	+	+	+	+	+		
18. Humor [Bm; JC; Jsk; Jns; FMP; FN; Lck; McG; TB; WM; WAW]	+		+	+		+	+	+	
19. Music, writing, arts [ER; Fg; GGG; Jhn86; Lck; LD; McG; Md; PB; SL; VY]	+		+	+	+	+			

Leadership

	1	2	3	4	5	6	7	8
20. Enjoyment of exploring environment [GGG; HS; JC; Lck; LD; M77; McG; SL; VY; WM]		+	+	+	+	+	+	+
21. Concern for peers [Brk; GGG; Jhn86; M82; McG; OB; SL; TB]			+	+	+	+	−	+
22. Sensitivity to others [GGG; Jhn86; Lck; McC; McG; Ptr; SKK; SL; TB; VY; Wt80; Wms]			+	+	+	+	+	+
23. Influence on others [Brk; GGG; Glg66; 72; GTP; Jhn70; Lck; M77; McC; GTP; OB; Sch; SL; VY]		+	+		+	+	+	+
24. Integration with peers [BO; CSW; DB; Dls88; EI; FN; GGG; Hys; Jns; Jsk; Ksh; Lbm; Lck; McC; McG; Mt; OB; Ptr; SKK; VY; WMK; Wt80]	−	−		−	−	−	−	−
25. Self-esteem [Dls88; ECW; GGG; Lck; M77; McG; Md; MS; SKK; VY; WMK]		−	+	−	−	−	−	−

Table 3 continued

Most Commonly Exhibited Traits of Gifted–Disabled Subpopulations

Ab	Abroms, 1988	HS	Harvey & Seeley, 1984	PB	Pollack & Branden, 1982
APL	Aaron, Phillips, & Larsen, 1988	JC	Johnsen & Corn, 1989	Ptr	Peterson, 1993
BLW	Bireley, Languis, & Williamson, 1992	Jhn70	Johnson, 1970	R	Rack, 1981
Bm	Baum, 1988	Jhn80	Johnson, 1980	RS	Rasner & Seymour, 1983
BMK	Bas, Mishra, & Kirby, 1994	Jhn86	Johnson, 1986	Sch	Schale, 1972, in Maker, 1977
BO	Baum & Owen, 1988	Jns	Jones, 1986	SH	Sloat & Hayes, 1990
Bty	Beaty, 1994	Jsk	Jansky, 1980	SKK	Schiff, Kaufman, & Kaufman, 1981
Bw	Bow, 1988	K54,55	Keller, 1954, 1955	SL	Stephenson & Leroux, 1994
CI	Coleman, 1992	Ksh	Kuschel, 1973, in Maker, 1977	Stv	Steeves, 1983
CP	Caplan & Powell, 1964, in Seeley, 1984	LD	Levey & Dolan, 1980, in Harvey & Seeley, 1984	T	Toll, 1993
Crn	Cornell, 1992			TB	Tannenbaum & Baldwin, 1983
CSW	Charlson, Strong, & Gold, 1993	Ldg	Lieding, 1981	U	Udall, 1985
DB	Dauber & Benbow, 1990	Lx	Leroux, 1986, in Sloat & Hayes, 1990	UM	Udall & Maker, 1983
Dls88	Delisle, 1988	M77	Maker, 1977	VY	Vespi & Yewchuk, 1992
Dls90	Delisle, 1990	M82	Maker, 1982	WAW	Whiting, Anderson, & Ward, 1980
ECW	Erin, Corn, & Wolffle, 1993	McC	McCants, 1985	Wg	Wingenbach, 1985
EI	Ellston, 1993	McG	McGreevey, 1992	WM	Whitmore & Maker, 1985
ER	Elrod & Ryckman, 1984	Md	Mindell, 1982	WMK	Whitmore, Maker, & Knott, 1985
FBT	Fox, Brody, & Tobin, 1983	Mhy	Mahoney, 1980, in Seeley, 1984	Wms	Williams, 1988
Fg	Fagerstrom, 1988	MS	Miner & Siegel, 1992	WS	Waldron & Saphire, 1990
FN	Fall & Nolan, 1993	Msh	Morishima, 1974	Wt80	Whitmore, 1980
FMP	Fleury, McNeil, & Pflaum, 1981	Mt	Mautner, 1984	Wt81	Whitmore, 1981
GGG	Goertzel, Goertzel, & Goertzel, 1978	NHHW	Nielsen, Higgins, Hammond, & Williams, 1993		
GGR	Gerber, Ginsberg, & Reiff, 1992				
GTP	Gath, Tenneth, & Pidduck, 1970	NK	Newcomb & Kilbourn, 1973		
HLW	Hollingworth, 1942, in Maker, 1977	OB	Osborne & Byrnes, 1990		

As seen in Table 3, a matrix of those traits shown by more than half the gifted-disabled groups (i.e., revealed by at least five of these nine groups) proves there is legitimate reason for positive academic expectations for gifted students with mild handicaps. In this matrix, a plus (+) means the pronounced presence of a trait, a minus (—) means the substantial deficit of a characteristic, and a blank means that there is no clear-cut, substantive literature discussion on that trait for that group. Gifted students with mild disabilities, you'll see, exhibit many pluses.

Learning

Despite the difficulties of the gifted mildly disabled in some basic skills, they have many of the prerequisites needed to excel in more complicated intellectual endeavors. Most gifted groups with mild disabilities have broad general knowledge.[9] While they may have extremely poor auditory memories in those areas of school study that do not interest them—phonics and math facts sometimes are two such areas[10]—they may demonstrate excellent recall for those matters that do intrigue them.[11]

Further, their oral expressive vocabularies may be outstanding.[12] In particular, gifted pupils with learning disabilities have been observed to use finely worded explanations to cover for their learning and behavioral shortcomings.[13] Gifted students with learning disabilities and communication disorders can often analyze and find explanations for those abstract and complicated problems presented in their school materials.[14]

Gifted pupils with mild disabilities may enjoy reading when presented with material at appropriate reading levels or with selections possessing interesting content.[15] And, to the extent that content is understood and enjoyed, decoding competence and reading comprehension can increase. One famous Hollywood actor with dyslexia said he knows when he has a potentially enjoyable role when the script "reads like gold."

In overall academic performance, grades may be average or above-average for gifted students with mild disabilities.[16] Learning problems with memory skills and other low-level intellectual competencies may diminish scholastic performance just enough, so that these highly capable students achieve mostly average grades and are not referred for either gifted or disability assessments. This scenario of hidden exceptionalities seems to be played out particularly frequently with high-potential learning disabled students.[17]

Some gifted pupils with mild disabilities may be inconsistent in their overall grades. But, while these students are variable in their performance across subjects, they tend to consistently express their particular strengths and weaknesses in specific subjects.[18]

Motivation

The motivational traits of gifted students with mild disabilities can be as complicated as their learning patterns. These students may lack persistence on rote classroom tasks, activities that may be as simple as handwriting exercises.[19] One explanation for this lack of persistence may be boredom with the simplicity of their activities.[20] Another reason might be that the tasks, which seem simple on the surface, require deeper exploration and turn out to be frustratingly difficult to accomplish, particularly for gifted LD students.[21] Ironically, despite their problems on seemingly simple tasks, the gifted mildly disabled often desire challenges in the higher realms of learning, such as Bloom's (1956) levels of analysis, synthesis, and evaluation.[22] Because of this desire, they may pursue their particular strengths and interests doggedly.[23]

Creativity

Creative endeavors are among the most determined pursuits of gifted students with mild disabilities. These pupils may solve problems with careful planning and ingenuity.[24] They may dream up humorous and clever jokes and stories,[25] and they may excel in any of a spectrum of musical, written, and visual arts.[26]

Leadership/Social Development

The leadership characteristics of gifted LD and ED students are perhaps more difficult to observe than their learning, motivational, and creative traits, perhaps because these characteristics involve interactions with other people, rather than just the interactions of the gifted LD or ED student with a task. To determine if an LD or ED student is a gifted leader, teachers must either be carefully on the lookout for leadership traits in pupils' daily classroom interactions or ask peers or parents if this student has leadership qualities (e.g., on the playground, in the community, or at home).[27] Many of these pupils enjoy exploring their environments,[28] sometimes to the point of stepping into society's "dark shadows" and discovering people and places that adults might prefer they not discover.[29]

Having suffered extensively themselves, these students can be very sensitive to the pain of peers.[30] On the other hand, gifted ED pupils may not demonstrate that kind of concern outwardly, or in the same way that gifted LD and gifted communication-disordered students do.[31] They also can act to redress perceived injustices inflicted on themselves and others. For example, gifted students with learning disabilities can articulately criticize "unfair" school policies.[32]

Unfortunately, the interpersonal and institutional concerns of gifted students with mild disabilities may not be reciprocated or even valued at all. Their influence on peers is often negative.[33] Gifted LD students, delinquents, and severe underachievers, in particular, may drive peers away with behavior perceived to be "demanding" or "strange."[34] Sadly, educators may regard these pupils' requests as attempts to usurp teacher authority.[35] Thus, both teachers and peers regard gifted pupils with mild disabilities as challenging.[36] In being negatively regarded by both groups, these students may have low self-esteem.[37]

Additional Traits of the Gifted Learning Disabled

The ironies observed in some of the behaviors of gifted children with mild disabilities are particularly apparent in gifted LD pupils, for whom additional, distinctive traits are listed in Tables 3 and 4. To paraphrase Winston Churchill (who was describing China of the mid-20th century), the gifted student with a learning disability in many ways can impress teachers as a "contradiction, hidden inside a riddle, wrapped in an enigma."

Learning

One contradiction in these students is that, in spite of their auditory and visual memory problems[38] (see Table 3), they can often obtain ample information through stories.[39] And, in spite of these difficulties in their "information-input" channels, they also can become highly aware of their own strengths and weaknesses[40] (see Table 4). Unfortunately, these students' intellectual skills and knowledge may be hidden from teachers, whose attention may be fixed on their gaping deficiencies,[41] rather than their strong subjects.[42]

Educators may be put off or unimpressed by knowledgeable, but detailed and wordy test-item responses.[43] And teachers may be puzzled, rather than be made hopeful, by these students' better performances on challenging activities than on easy tasks.[44] They may wonder, for example, how these students know the answers to upper-level science and math questions,[45] but have difficulty in spelling those answers.

Gifted pupils with learning disabilities do have a number of academic strengths that will shine through to discerning teachers, though. In addition to higher-level math and science, they may have good reading comprehension skills in various subjects, due to their broad background knowledge and varied interests,[46] and due to their self-correction of decoding and comprehension errors.[47] Their insight into people's motives also may be an asset.[48]

Table 4

Additional Traits of the Gifted Learning Disabled

Learning	Motivation
1. Awareness of strengths, weaknesses [BO; Bw; Md; Mt; SR; Stv; Wms; Wg; WMK]	20. Poor attention [BLW; BO; D; Jns; TB]
2. Hidden knowledge base [TB]	21. Poor organization [BLW; SKK; VY; WMK]
3. Strong in one or more school subjects [T]	22. Sluggish class work [BO; BLW; Jns; VY]
4. More information than is required on tests [EI]	23. Sensitivity to criticism [NHHW]
5. Better performance on harder tasks [BLW]	24. Excuses for poor performance [MS]
6. Competence in upper-level math and science [MS; NHHW]	25. Independent task approach [R]
7. Interest in big picture surrounding lesson [NHHW]	26. Excitability on strong interests [BLW]
8. Error detection in decoding reading [HS]	27. Concern about present, future achievements [Mt; TB; WMK]
9. Insight [NHHW]	28. Benefits from advice on learning style [FN]
10. Learning problems increase over time [EI; NHHW]	29. Guilt about shortcuts [WMK]
11. Repeated grades [VY]	
12. Speech problems [DMK; VY]	
13. Decoding problems [DMK]	
14. Poor spelling [FN; T]	
15. Poor handwriting, written composition [BLW; EI; FN; MS; T; VY]	
16. Vision problems [BLW]	
17. Reversing and sequencing difficulties [APL; Bw; Jsk; PB; WMK]	
18. Poor eye-hand coordination [Mt; Wms]	
19. Ear infections, allergies, stomach aches [EI; T; VY]	

Creativity

30. Curiosity about unfamiliar [EI; NHHW; WMK]
31. Combining unusual ideas [Bm; BO; EI; TB; WMK]
32. Self-modification on academic tasks [EI; Mt; Wg; WMK]
33. Thought-provoking comments [RS]
34. Daydreaming [EI; MS]
35. Self-designed experiments [NHHW]
36. Creative masking of disability [T]
37. Creation of own environment to excel, support [EI; GGR; MS]

Leadership

38. Manipulativeness [TB]
39. Oral language skills as compensation [T]
40. Boring lectures to classmates [TB]
41. Criticisms of school policies [TB]
42. Classroom disruptiveness [BLW; D; FN; TB]
43. Feelings of helplessness [BO; PB; T; VY]
44. Withdrawal [BO; Hys; Jns; Jsk; Mt; SKK; Wt; WMK]
45. Varied outside hobbies, interests [EI; T]
46. Good mechanical skills [Hys]
47. Good sports performance [Jsk; NHHW; PB; VY]
48. Potential in military or business [GGR]
49. Benefits from advice of gifted peers [FN]
50. Supportive family [EI; R; VY]
51. Parents and teachers puzzled by disability [T; VY]

APL	Aaron, Phillips, & Larsen, 1988
BLW	Bireley, Languis, & Williamson, 1992
Bm	Baum, 1988
Bo	Baum & Owen, 1988
Bw	Bow, 1988
D	Denckla, 1988
DMK	Das, Mishra, & Kirby, 1994
EI	Ellston, 1983
FN	Fall & Nolan, 1993
GGR	Gerber, Ginsberg, & Reiff, 1992
HS	Hannah & Shore, 1995
Hys	Hayes, 1980
Jns	Jones, 1986
Jsk	Jansky, 1980
Md	Mindell, 1982

MS	Miner & Siegel, 1992
Mt	Mautner, 1984
NHHW	Nielsen, Higgins, Hammond, & Williams, 1993
PB	Pollack & Branden, 1982
R	Rack, 1981
RS	Rosner & Seymour, 1983
SKK	Schiff, Kaufman, & Kaufman, 1981
T	Toll, 1992
TB	Tannenbaum & Baldwin, 1983
VY	Vespi & Yewchuk, 1992
Wg	Wingenbach, 1985
WMK	Whitmore, Maker, & Knott, 1985
Wms	Williams, 1988
Wt	Whitmore, 1980

Sadly, basic-skills deficits of gifted pupils with disabilities tend to compound over time,[49] particularly in language skills. These increasing problems leave these students with poorer school marks than they are capable of earning and occasionally cause them to repeat grades.[50] Skill deficits may occur, particularly in speech,[51] decoding,[52] spelling,[53] and handwriting and written composition.[54]

In addition to deficient basic skills, gifted LD pupils' grades may be lowered by the following problems: poor eyesight;[55] reversing or sequencing difficulties with letters, words, and numbers;[56] eye-hand coordination problems;[57] and school days missed due to ear infections, allergies, and stomach aches.[58]

Motivation

Another complexity in this group (see Table 4) is that gifted LD students, in spite of their great potential and desire to do well, display a number of consistent, nagging learning difficulties, including poor attention[59] and haphazard organization.[60] These problems may lead to sluggishly or incorrectly done work.[61]

Gifted LD students' reactions to their learning problems may compound these difficulties. They may react oversensitively to criticism of their work[62] and give excuses for poor performance,[63] both of which may alienate their teachers (Table 4).

Gifted pupils with learning disabilities are not stopped dead in their tracks by teacher disapproval, however. They can display strong and highly personal motives in pursuing their school assignments. As evidenced in Table 4, some of these pupils may desire to use independent, rather unusual, task-approach styles,[64] and may carry them out with great zeal as "their own inventions."[65] Others may have concerns about their present academic achievement or future job prospects,[66] and may seek advice on effective study strategies from gifted peers.[67] Gifted LD students also may worry about the viability or appropriateness of their own shortcuts in performing academic tasks.[68]

Creativity

While their desire to achieve in traditional academic pursuits may be surprising to some teachers, the strong motivation of gifted LD students to be creative probably raises fewer eyebrows. As suggested by Table 4, their creative problem-solving ingenuity may be based in part on a curiosity about the unknown.[69] They often try to solve problems by combining ideas not usually joined.[70] One frequently observed type of problem solving is an industrious, ongoing search for self-modification of their approaches to academic tasks, after ineffective strategies have been employed.[71]

Devising creative task-approach strategies is just one way in which the gifted learning disabled combine unusual ideas. Their ideas also may be presented in thought-provoking classroom comments throughout the school day[72] (Table 4), in picturesque, daydreamy oral or written stories in language arts classes,[73] or in self-designed scientific experiments.[74]

Gifted LD students' innovative strategies are just one way that they can utilize their strengths, partially mask their disabilities,[75] and create an environment that includes some disability-sensitive parents, teachers, and assignments[76] (Table 4).

Leadership/Social Development

As tied up as they may be in creative endeavors and scholastic frustrations, gifted pupils with learning disabilities may not be popular with peers or teachers (Table 4). Classmates and educators may be put off by gifted LD students, as they witness these pupils sometimes manipulating their teachers and peers,[77] using advanced vocabulary to impress others,[78] lecturing classmates in boring fashion,[79] delivering open criticisms of school policies,[80] and disrupting classroom activities.[81] Social rejection, combined with academic failure, may lead to feelings of helplessness,[82] depression,[83] and eventual social withdrawal.[84]

Gifted pupils with learning disabilities may build a more positive self-image by excelling in varied, out-of-school hobbies and interests[85] (Table 4). They may excel particularly in mechanics[86] and athletics[87]— two sets of psychomotor capabilities that surprisingly are not precluded by the eye-hand coordination problems that often plague gifted LD pupils' academic work.[88] These students also may begin talking enthusiastically about career intentions, such as in business or the military.[89] Gifted LD students may be bolstered in their self-esteem and career plans by the advice of gifted peers[90] and the support of loving,[91] but sometimes puzzled or exasperated,[92] parents.

Additional Traits of the Gifted Emotionally Disturbed

High-potential LD pupils, like other gifted-disabled groups, certainly can diverge from one another in their traits. Gifted students with emotional disabilities can differ particularly extensively from one another in their characteristics. It is important for readers not to expect to see all the traits listed below from all members of all the distinctive, high-potential ED groups—withdrawn and depressed pupils, suicidal students, substantial underachievers with behavioral problems, and delinquents. Instead, it is important to know which gifted ED group shows which characteristics, and to observe each potentially gifted group accordingly.

Learning

Table 3 indicates that gifted-suicidal students and gifted-delinquent pupils may have difficulties, first in distancing themselves from, and then in analytically overviewing, those interpersonal struggles in which they are involved.[93] They may concentrate on the interpersonal trees rather than the forests in addressing these problems.[94]

In addition, as Table 5 shows, delinquents may have a disproportionate share of learning disabilities,[95] although they may quickly solve problems in those subjects in which they are strong.[96] Further, while they may have suffered through unsuccessful academic and social interventions in the past,[97] they have the capability of making up deficits in strong subjects quickly, if they are "turned on" in a particular course.[98]

Motivation

As evidenced in Table 5, suicidal pupils also may be very well organized to accomplish those academic tasks at which they excel.[99] On the other hand, they have much more difficulty in organizing their responses to their troublesome school-related activities, just as they have problems in developing responses to their personal dilemmas. Delinquents and underachievers may miss a good deal of school,[100] and they may be overly active[101] or silent and morbid[102] when they do attend. Suicidal pupils may express fear of failure,[103] and may demonstrate perfectionism in their academic work.[104]

Creativity

As suggested by Table 3, one reason that delinquents and suicidal youth have trouble solving their personal difficulties is the rigidity of their problem-solving approaches.[105]

In other activities, ones by which they are not personally consumed (see Table 5), they may exhibit a number of right-brain traits. These traits, which are frequently attributed to children with learning disabilities, include nonverbal perceptiveness,[106] intuitive comments,[107] holistic thinking,[108] mood shifts[109] fantasizing,[110] and thrill-seeking behavior.[111]

To insulate themselves against the firestorms of social ire that go with a right-brain personality, these students may surround themselves with a circle of unusual, but supportive, friends from different backgrounds than their own.[112] They also may devise their own stress-relieving outlooks on life[113] (Table 5).

Leadership/Social Development

Gifted delinquents may be distinguished from the gifted learning disabled by their years-long pattern of lesser concern for school peers. As evidenced in Table 3, gifted delinquents, like high-potential under-achievers, may show little outward concern for their fellow students,[114] despite possibly identifying with these classmates' pain.[115]

As part of a generally assertive pattern of behavior[116] alluded to in Table 5, these students may demonstrate intolerance toward less able peers.[117] They also may question and manipulate rules,[118] and rebel publicly and privately against authority.[119] Although delinquents may rise assertively to leadership positions within their particular circles of friends,[120] gifted students with emotional disabilities as a group generally experience difficulty in adapting to social settings.[121]

The school-based social difficulties of gifted-disturbed students appear to develop and strengthen over a period of years. While some parents and communities do a very good job of trying to nurture and connect with these students, at other times these pupils' problems clearly may be due to out-of-school factors. Some gifted delinquents may have experienced neglectful or abusive homes,[122] or foster homes for which they felt little attachment.[123] Even in relatively stable families, gifted delinquents or gifted-suicidal students may operate in a swirl of conflict.[124]

As gifted pupils with emotional disabilities grow older, change schools, lose some familiar friends, and face impersonal and otherwise challenging surroundings, teachers may notice substantially increased anger or depression.[125] They may react to their troubled pasts and threatening new environments with nonviolent offenses like curfew violations, substance use, or theft.[126] They may even engage in self-mutilation or suicide attempts.[127]

On a positive note—and unlike a number of disturbed pupils who are not gifted—gifted students who are depressed or delinquent have shown that they can markedly improve their own fates. While they are uncertain about what makes them special,[128] they often believe that they are destined for outstanding achievements.[129] Some even dedicate themselves to making the world better for other people through working on truth and justice issues.[130]

Additional Traits of the Gifted Communication Disordered

The literature on gifted communication-disordered students (those with substantial speech and language impairments) resembles the literature on gifted LD students in many respects.

Learning

Gifted students with communication disorders may be intrigued with visual patterns in puzzles and mazes [131] (Table 6). However, in

Table 5

Additional Traits of the Gifted Emotionally Disturbed

Learning	Motivation
1. Learning disability [Brk]	5. Good self-organization [Dls88; McC]
2. Quick problem-solving [HS; Sy; Wt 81]	6. Poor, half-hearted school attendance [GTP; KAT]
3. Varied, unsuccessful interventions [NHHW]	7. Overactivity [GGG]
4. Quick make-up of deficits [OB]	8. Fear of failure, seeming downcast [Dls88; GGG; Hm; Lck]
	9. Perfectionism [DIs; McC]

Brk	Brooks, 1972, in Seeley, 1984	Jhn70	Johnson, 1970, cited in Lajoie & Shore, 1981
Crn	Cornell, 1992	KAT	Kolko, Ayllon, & Torrence, 1987
Dls88	Delisle, 1988		
GGG	Goertzel, Goertzel, & Goertzel, 1978	Lck	Lovecky, 1992
		M82	Maker, 1982
Glg66,72	Gallagher, 1966, 1972	McC	McCants, 1985
GTP	Gath, Tenneth, & Pidduck, 1970, cited in Lajoie & Shore, 1981	Mhy	Mahoney, 1980, in Seeley, 1984
		OB	Osborne & Byrnes, 1990
Hlw	Hollingworth, 1942	Ptr	Peterson, 1993
Hm	Hermanson & LeDew, 1958, in Maker, 1977	SH	Sloat & Hayes, 1990
		Sy	Seeley, 1984
HS	Harvey & Seeley, 1984	Wt81	Whitmore, 1981

Creativity

10. Nonverbal perceptiveness [HS; Lck; OB; Sy]
11. Intuition [Jhn 70; Lck; NHHW]
12. Holistic thinking [Lck; NHHW]
13. Mood shifts [GGG; Ptr; SH]
14. Fantasies [Lck; Ptr]
15. Thrill-seeking behavior [GGG; Ptr]
16. Unlikely friends [Lck]
17. Create barriers against stress [Crn; Ptr]

Leadership

18. Assertiveness (for better, worse) [Lck; M82; OB]
19. Intolerance toward less-able [Hlw]
20. Questions about, manipulations of rules [Brk; Crn; Lck; Glg66, 72; M77; McC; NHHW]
21. Public, private rebellion against authority [Brk; Dls88; Hlw; Lck; OB; Ptr]
22. Leadership among friends [Jhn70; OB; Ptr]
23. Difficulties in adapting socially [Dls88; GGG; Lck; M82; OB]
24. Neglectful and abusive homes [OB]
25. Foster homes [OB]
26. Home conflict [Crn; OB; SH]
27. Poor school-to-school transition [OB]
28. Deep anger or depression [Ptr]
29. Substance-use, theft, and other nonviolent offenses [Crn; OB; SH]
30. Self-mutilation [Ptr]
31. Suicide attempts [SH]
32. Uncertain about why different [Lck]
33. Sense of destiny for excellence [Lck; OB; Ptr]
34. Concern with truth, fairness, and justice [Lck]

Table 6

Additional Traits of the Gifted Communication Disordered

Learning	Motivation	Creativity	Leadership
1. Interest in visual patterns [McG]	6. Seeking explanations [McG; NHHW]	7. Insight into relationships [McG; NHHW]	10. Cautious about involvement in social activities [NHHW]
2. Interest in "the big picture" [NHHW]		8. Exaggerations, fantasies [McG]	11. Sensitivity to criticism [NHHW]
3. Problems in "comprehending the print" [NHHW]		9. Stories to amuse others [McG]	12. Self-amusement [McG]
4. Stammering [McG]			13. Nurtured by, and nurturing of, family [McG]
5. Discrepancy between verbal and nonverbal skills [NHHW]			

McG McGreevey, 1992
NHHW Nielsen, Higgins, Hammond, & Williams, 1993

addition to their very particular interests inside and outside school, gifted communication-disordered students are intrigued with the "big picture" of interrelationships among the varied elements of knowledge about which they are learning.[132]

Unfortunately, like gifted LD pupils, in complicated listening and reading tasks, they may not comprehend the complicated language.[133] Some gifted pupils with speech impairments may stammer out their responses,[134] particularly under pressure. Some of these students may prefer written, gestured, or pictorial responses to oral answers.[135]

Motivation

Inquisitive speech-and-language-impaired pupils may seek further explanations on topics—topics in which they are either experts or are struggling.[136]

Creativity

Similar to gifted learning-disabled students, high-potential students with communication disorders may have particularly creative, insightful explanations for mathematical and human relationships—insights that they may articulate in nontraditional fashions or not at all.[137]

They may spend a good amount of time communicating with themselves, rather than with their same-age peers. They sometimes may engage in exaggerations or fantasies and tell others about these stories.[138]

Leadership

Gifted students with speech or language impairments may be less active socially than they are in their own worlds.[139] This isolation may be due to sensitivity over others' criticisms of their speech or writing.[140] In lieu of interacting with others, they may amuse themselves or they may spend time with supportive families,[141] as high-potential students with learning disabilities do.

Notes

1. Ysseldyke, J., Algozzine, B., & Thurlow, M. (1992). *Critical issues in special education* (2nd ed.). Boston: Houghton-Mifflin.
2. Bricklin, P. M. (1983). Working with parents of learning-disabled/gifted children. In L. H. Fox, L. Brody, & D. Tobin (Eds.), *Learning-disabled/gifted children: Identification and programming* (pp. 243–260). Baltimore: University Park Press.
3. Bricklin, 1983; Ciha, T. E. (1974). Parents as identifiers of giftedness: Ignored but accurate. *Gifted Child Quarterly, 18*, 191–195.
4. Senf, 1983.
5. Bricklin, 1983;
   Whitmore & Maker, 1985.
6. Senf, 1983.
7. Wang, M. C., Reynolds, M. C., & Walberg, H. J. (1986). Rethinking special education. *Educational Leadership, 44*(1), 26–31; Will, M. (1986). *Educating children with learning problems: A shared responsibility*. Washington, DC: U.S. Department of Education, Office of Special Education.
8. Will, 1986;
   U.S. Department of Education. (1987). *What works: Research about teaching and learning* (2nd ed.). Washington, DC: Office of Educational Research and Improvement.
9. McGreevey, A. (1992). All in the golden afternoon: The early life of Charles L. Dodgson (Lewis Carroll). *Gifted Child Quarterly, 36*, 6–10; Nielsen et al., 1993;
   Stephenson, D., & Leroux, J. A. (1994). Portrait of a creatively gifted child facing cancer. *Creativity Research Journal, 7*, 71–77;
   Tannenbaum, A. J., & Baldwin, L. J. (1983). Giftedness and learning disability: A paradoxical combination. In L. H. Fox, L. Brody, & D. Tobin (Eds.), *Learning-disabled/gifted children: Identification and programming* (pp. 11–36). Baltimore: University Park Press;
   Whitmore, J. R., & Maker, C. J., & Knott, G. (1985). Intellectually gifted persons with specific learning disabilities. In J. R. Whitmore & C. J. Maker, *Intellectual giftedness in disabled persons* (pp. 175–206). Rockville, MD: Aspen.
10. Maker, C. J. (1982). *Curriculum development for the gifted*. Rockville, MD: Aspen;
    Steeves, K. J. (1983). Memory as a factor in the computational efficiency of dyslexic children with high abstract reasoning ability. *Annals of Dyslexia, 33*, 141–152.
11. Maker, 1982;
    McGreevey, 1992;
    Whitmore et al., 1985.

12. Dauber, S. L., & Benbow, C. P. (1990). Aspects of personality and peer relations of extremely talented adolescents. *Gifted Child Quarterly, 34*, 10–15;

    Fall, J., & Nolan, L. (1993, January/February). A paradox of exceptionalities. *Gifted Child Today, 16*(1), 46–49;

    Goertzel, M. G., Goertzel, V., & Goertzel, T. (1978). *300 eminent personalities*. San Francisco: Jossey-Bass;

    Maker, 1982;

    McGreevey, 1992;

    Miner, M., & Siegel, L.S. (1992). William Butler Yeats: Dyslexic? *Journal of Learning Disabilities, 25*, 372–375;

    Peterson, J. (1993, January/February). What we learned from Jenna. *Gifted Child Today, 16*(1), 15–16;

    Tannenbaum & Baldwin, 1983;

    Vespi, L., & Yewchuk, C. (1992). A phenomenological study of the social/emotional characteristics of gifted learning disabled children. *Journal for the Education of the Gifted, 16,* 55–72.
13. Tannenbaum & Baldwin, 1983.
14. Fall & Nolan, 1993;

    Levey, S., & Dolan, J. (1988, May/June). Addressing specific learning disabilities in gifted students. *Gifted Child Today, 11*(3) 10–11;

    McGreevey, 1992;

    Neilsen et al., 1993;

    Steeves, 1983;

    Rosner, S. L., & Seymour, J. (1983). The gifted child with a learning disability: Clinical evidence. In L. H. Fox, L. Brody, & D. Tobin (Eds.), *Learning-disabled/gifted children: Identification and programming* (pp. 77–97). Baltimore: University Park Press;

    Waldron, K. A., & Saphire, D. G. (1990). An analysis of WISC-R factors for gifted students with learning disabilities. *Journal of Learning Disabilities, 23,* 491–498.
15. Aaron, P. G., Phillips, S., & Larsen, S. (1988). Specific reading disability in historically famous persons. *Journal of Learning Disabilities, 21*, 523–538;

    Gath, D., Tenneth, G., & Pidduck, R. (1970). Educational characteristics of bright delinquents. *British Journal of Educational Psychology, 40,* 216–219;

    Mautner, T. S. (1984). Dyslexia—my "invisible handicap." *Bulletin of the Orton Society, 34*, 299–311;

    McCants, G. (1985, May/June). Suicide and the gifted. *G/C/T, 8*(3), 27–29;

    McGreevey, 1992;

    Miner & Siegel, 1992;

    Williams, K. (1988). The learning-disabled gifted: An unmet challenge. *Gifted Child Quarterly, 11*, 17–18.

16. Abroms, K. (1978). Gifted and learning disabled. *G/C/T*, *1*(2), 26–28;
    Caplan, N. S., & Powell, M. A. (1964). A comparison of average to superior IQ delinquents. *Journal of Psychology*, *54*, 307–318;
    Dauber & Benbow, 1990;
    Ellston, T. (1993, January/February). Gifted and learning-disabled ... A paradox? *Gifted Child Today*, *16*(1), 17–19;
    Johnson, 1986;
    McGreevey, 1992;
    Senf, 1983;
    Sloat & Hayes, 1990.
17. Senf, 1983.
18. Caplan & Powell, 1964, in Seeley, 1984;
    Goertzel et al., 1978; Johnson, L. (1987). Comment: Teaching the visually impaired gifted youngster. *Journal of Visual Impairment and Blindness, 81,* 51–52;
    McGreevey, 1992;
    Peterson, 1993.
19. Bireley, M. M., Williamson, T., & Languis, M. (1992). Physiological uniqueness: A new perspective on the learning disabled/gifted child. *Roeper Review, 15*, 101–107;
    Dauber & Benbow, 1990;
    Ellston, 1993;
    Fall & Nolan, 1993;
    Goertzel et al., 1978;
    Hollingworth, L. S. (1942). *Children with above 180 IQ.* Yonkers-on-Hudson, NY: World Book;
    Johnson, 1986;
    Mahoney, A. R. (1980). Gifted delinquents: What do we know about them? *Child and Youth Services Review, 2*, 315–330;
    Miner & Siegel, 1992;
    Nielsen et al., 1993;
    Tannenbaum & Baldwin, 1983.
20. Hollingworth, 1942, in Maker, 1977.
21. Baum, 1988;
    Baum & Owen, 1988;
    Ellston, 1993;
    Fall & Nolan, 1993;
    Nielsen et al., 1993;
    Miner & Siegel, 1992;
    Tannenbaum & Baldwin, 1983.
22. Gerber, P. J., Ginsberg, R., & Reiff, H. B. (1992). Identifying alterable patterns in employment success for highly successful adults with learning disabilities. *Journal of Learning Disabilities, 25*, 475–487;

Goertzel, et al., 1978;
Hollingworth, 1942, in Maker, 1977;
McGreevey, 1992;
Nielsen et al., 1993.
23. Baum, 1988;
Baum & Owen, 1988;
Fall & Nolan, 1993;
Fox, Brody, & Tobin, 1983;
Gerber, Ginsberg, & Reiff, 1992;
Goertzel et al., 1978;
Jones, B. (1986). The gifted dyslexic. *Annals of Dyslexia, 36*, 301–317;
Jansky, J. J. (1980). Language disability: A case study. *Annals of Dyslexia, 30*, 252–267;
Mahoney, 1980, in Seeley, 1984;
McGreevey, 1992;
Miner & Siegel, 1992;
Rack, L. (1981). Developmental dyslexia and literary creativity in the area of deficit. *Journal of Learning Disabilities, 14*, 262–263;
Udall, A. (1985). Chapter reaction. In J. R. Whitmore & C.J. Maker, *Intellectual giftedness in disabled persons* (pp. 207–209). Rockville, MD: Aspen.
24. Coleman, M. R. (1992). A comparison of how gifted/LD and average/LD boys cope with school frustration. *Journal for the Education of the Gifted, 15*, 239–265;
Delisle, J. (1990). The gifted adolescent at risk: Strategies and resources for suicide prevention. *Journal for the Education of the Gifted, 13*, 212–228;
Johnson, 1986;
McGreevey, 1992;
Nielsen et al., 1993.
25. Baum, 1988;
Fall & Nolan, 1993;
Jansky, 1980;
Lovecky, D. V. (1992). Exploring social and emotional aspects of giftedness in children. *Roeper Review, 15*, 18–25;
McGreevey, 1992.
26. Ryckman, D. B., & Elrod, E. F. (1984). Once is not enough. *Journal of Learning Disabilities, 16*, 87–89;
Lovecky, 1992;
Levey, S., & Dolan, J., 1988;
Harvey, S., & Seeley, K. R. (1984). An investigation of the relationships among intellectual and creative abilities, extracurricular activities, achievement and giftedness in a delinquent population. *Gifted Child Quarterly, 28*, 73–79;
McGreevey, 1992;

Mindell, P. (1982). The gifted dyslexic: A case study with theoretical and educational implications. *Roeper Review, 4*(3), 22–23; Vespi & Yewchuk, 1992.

27. Davis & Rimm, 1985.
28. Goertzel et al., 1978;
    Levey & Dolan, 1988;
    Lovecky, 1992;
    McGreevey, 1992;
    Vespi & Yewchuk, 1992.
29. Harvey & Seeley, 1984.
30. Goertzel et al., 1978;
    McCants, 1985;
    McGreevey, 1992;
    Peterson, 1993;
    Schiff et al., 1981;
    Vespi & Yewchuk, 1992;
    Whitmore, 1980;
    Williams, 1988.
31. Goertzel et al., 1978;
    Maker, 1982;
    McGreevey, 1992;
    Osborne & Byrnes, 1990;
    Tannenbaum & Baldwin, 1983.
32. Tannenbaum & Baldwin, 1983.
33. Gallagher, P. A. (1966). *An art media procedure for developing creativity in emotionally disturbed children.* Unpublished master's thesis, University of Kansas, Lawrence;
    Gallagher, P. A. (1972). Procedures for developing creativity in emotionally disturbed children. *Focus on Exceptional Children, 4,* 1–9;
    Lovecky, 1992;
    Maker, C. J. (1977). *Providing programs for the gifted handicapped.* Reston, VA: Council for Exceptional Children;
    McCants, 1985;
    Vespi & Yewchuk, 1992.
34. Baum & Owen, 1988;
    Goertzel et al., 1978;
    Osborne & Byrnes, 1990;
    Whitmore, 1980.
35. Tannenbaum & Baldwin, 1983.
36. Baum & Owen, 1988;
    Dauber & Benbow, 1990;
    Delisle, 1988;
    Ellston, 1993;
    Fall & Nolan, 1993;
    Goertzel et al., 1978;

Hayes, G. W. (1984). Unlocking the dyslexic teenage reader: Paul's gift. *Annals of Dyslexia, 28*, 186–193;
Jansky, 1980;
Lovecky, 1992;
Mautner, 1984;
McCants, 1985;
McGreevey, 1992;
Schiff et al., 1981;
Whitmore, 1980;
Whitmore et al., 1985.
37. Delisle, 1988;
Ellston, 1993;
Lovecky, 1992;
McGreevey, 1992;
Mindell, 1982;
Miner & Siegel, 1992;
Schiff et al., 1981;
Vespi & Yewchuk, 1992;
Whitmore et al., 1985.
38. Whitmore et al., 1985.
39. Weaver, P. A., & Dickinson, D. K. (1979). Story comprehension and recall in dyslexic students. *Bulletin of the Orton Society*, 157–171.
40. Baum & Owen, 1988;
Bow, J. N. (1988). A comparison of intellectually superior male reading achievers and underachievers from a neuropsychological perspective. *Journal of Learning Disabilities, 21*, 118–123;
Mautner, 1984;
Mindell, 1982;
Rosner & Seymour, 1983;
Steeves, 1983;
Williams, 1988;
Wingenbach, N. (1985). Chapter reaction (to "Intellectually gifted persons with specific learning disabilities"). In J. R. Whitmore & C. J. Maker (Eds.), *Intellectual giftedness in disabled persons* (pp. 210–211). Rockville, MD: Aspen;
Whitmore et al., 1985.
41. Tannenbaum & Baldwin, 1983.
42. Toll, M. F. (1993, January/February). Gifted learning-disabled: A kaleidoscope of needs. *Gifted Child Today, 16*(1), 34–35.
43. Ellston, 1993.
44. Bireley et al., 1992.
45. Miner & Siegel, 1992;
Nielsen et al., 1993.
46. Nielsen et al., 1993.

47. Hannah, C. L., & Shore, B. M. (1995). Metacognition and high intellectual ability: Insights from the study of learning-disabled gifted students. *Gifted Child Quarterly, 39*, 95–109.
48. Nielsen et al., 1993.
49. Nielsen et al., 1993.
50. Vespi & Yewchuk, 1992.
51. Das, J. P., Mishra, R. K., & Kirby, J. R. (1994). Cognitive patterns of children with dyslexia: A comparison between groups with high and average non-verbal intelligence. *Journal of Learning Disabilities, 27*, 235–242;
    Vespi & Yewchuk, 1992.
52. Das et al., 1994.
53. Fall & Nolan, 1993;
    Toll, 1993.
54. Bireley et al., 1992;
    Ellston, 1993;
    Fall & Nolan, 1993;
    Miner & Siegel, 1992;
    Toll, 1992;
    Vespi & Yewchuk, 1992.
55. Bireley et al., 1992.
56. Aaron et al., 1988;
    Bow, 1988;
    Jansky, 1980;
    Pollack, C., & Branden, A. (1982). Odyssey of a "mirrored" personality. *Annals of Dyslexia, 32*, 275–288;
    Whitmore et al., 1985.
57. Mautner, 1984;
    Williams, 1988.
58. Ellston, 1993;
    Toll, 1993;
    Yewchuk & Vespi, 1992.
59. Baum & Owen, 1988;
    Bireley et al., 1992;
    Denckla, M. (1988). Cited in "Myelin deposits affect brain activity, higher-level thinking." *TAG Update, 11*(3), 1;
    Jones, 1986;
    Tannenbaum & Baldwin, 1983.
60. Bireley et al., 1992;
    Schiff et al., 1981;
    Vespi & Yewchuk, 1992;
    Whitmore et al., 1985.
61. Baum & Owen, 1988;
    Bireley et al., 1992;
    Jones, 1986;

Vespi & Yewchuk, 1992.

62. Nielsen et al., 1993.
63. Miner & Siegel, 1992.
64. Rack, 1981.
65. Bireley et al., 1992.
66. Baum, 1988;
    Mautner, 1984;
    Tannenbaum & Baldwin, 1983;
    Whitmore et al., 1985.
67. Fall & Nolan, 1993.
68. Whitmore et al., 1985.
69. Ellston, 1993;
    Nielsen et al., 1992;
    Whitmore et al., 1985.
70. Baum, 1988;
    Baum & Owen, 1988;
    Ellston, 1993;
    Tannenbaum & Baldwin, 1983;
    Whitmore et al., 1985.
71. Ellston, 1993;
    Mautner, 1984;
    Whitmore et al., 1985;
    Wingenbach, 1985.
72. Rosner & Seymour, 1983.
73. Ellston, 1993;
    Miner & Siegel, 1992.
74. Nielsen et al., 1992.
75. Toll, 1993.
76. Ellston, 1993;
    Gerber et al., 1992;
    Miner & Siegel, 1992.
77. Tannenbaum & Baldwin, 1983.
78. Toll, 1993.
79. Tannenbaum, & Baldwin, 1983.
80. Tannenbaum & Baldwin, 1983.
81. Bireley et al., 1992;
    Denckla, 1988;
    Fall & Nolan, 1993;
    Tannenbaum & Baldwin, 1983.
82. Baum & Owen, 1983;
    Pollack & Branden, 1982;
    Toll, 1993;
    Vespi & Yewchuk, 1992.
83. Ellston, 1993;
    Fall & Nolan, 1993;

Vespi & Yewchuk, 1992.

84. Baum & Owen, 1988;
    Hayes, 1978;
    Jansky, 1980;
    Jones, 1986;
    Mautner, 1984;
    Schiff, Kaufman, & Kaufman, 1981;
    Whitmore, 1980;
    Whitmore, Maker, & Knott, 1985.

85. Ellston, 1993;
    Toll, 1993.

86. Hayes, 1978.

87. Jansky, 1980;
    Nielsen et al., 1993;
    Pollack & Branden, 1982;
    Vespi & Yewchuk, 1992.

88. Pollack & Branden, 1982.

89. Gerber et al., 1992.

90. Fall & Nolan, 1993.

91. Ellston, 1993;
    Rack, 1981;
    Vespi & Yewchuk, 1992.

92. Toll, 1993;
    Vespi & Yewchuk, 1992.

93. Goertzel et al., 1978;
    Maker, 1982.

94. Osborne & Byrnes, 1990.

95. Parker, H. K. (1970). On making incorrigible youths corrigible. *Journal of Secondary Education, 45*, 57–60.

96. Harvey & Seeley, 1984;
    Seeley, K.R. (1984). Perspectives on adolescent giftedness and delinquency. *Journal for the Education of the Gifted, 8*, 59–72;
    Whitmore, J. R. (1981). Gifted children with handicapping conditions: A new frontier. *Exceptional Children, 48*, 106–114.

97. Nielsen et al., 1993.

98. Osborne & Byrnes, 1990.

99. Delisle, 1988;
    McCants, 1985.

100. Gath, Tenneth, & Pidduck, 1970;
    Kolko, D. J., Ayllon, T., & Torrence, C. (1987). Positive practice routines in overcoming resistance to the treatment of school phobia: A case study with follow-up. *Journal of Behavior Therapy and Experimental Psychiatry, 18*, 249–253.

101. Goertzel et al., 1978.

102. Lovecky, 1991.

103. Delisle, 1988;
     Goertzel et al., 1978;
     Hermanson, D., & LaDew, H. (1958). Some psychological and psychiatric findings on gifted students in San Diego. Unpublished manuscript cited in C. J. Maker (1977), *Providing programs for the gifted handicapped* (Reston, VA: Council for Exceptional Children).
104. Delisle, 1988;
     McCants, 1985.
105. Delisle, 1988;
     Goertzel et al., 1978.
106. Harvey & Seeley, 1984;
     Seeley, 1984.
107. Johnson, D. E. (1970). Personality characteristics in relation to college persistence. *Journal of Counseling Psychology, 17*, 162–167.
108. Lovecky, 1992;
     Nielsen et al., 1993.
109. Goertzel et al., 1978;
     Hayes, M. L., & Sloat, R. S. (1990). Suicide and the gifted adolescent. *Journal for the Education of the Gifted, 13*, 239–244;
     Peterson, 1993.
110. Lovecky, 1991;
     Peterson, 1993.
111. Goertzel et al., 1978;
     Peterson, 1993.
112. Lovecky, 1992.
113. Cornell, 1992;
     Peterson, 1993.
114. Goertzel et al., 1978;
     Maker, 1982.
115. Goertzel et al., 1978;
     McCants, 1985.
116. Lovecky, 1992;
     Maker, 1982;
     Osborne & Byrnes, 1990.
117. Hollingworth, 1942.
118. Brooks, P. (1972). *Bright delinquents: The story of a unique school.* London: The National Foundation for Educational Research in England & Wales;
     Cornell, D. G. (1992). High intelligence and severe delinquency: Evidence disputing the connection. *Roeper Review, 14*, 233–239;
     Gallagher, 1966, 1972;
     Lovecky, 1992;
     Maker, 1977;
     McCants, 1985;
     Nielsen et al., 1993.

119. Brooks, 1972;
Delisle, 1988;
Hollingworth, 1942;
Lovecky, 1992;
Osborne & Byrnes, 1990;
Peterson, 1993.
120. Johnson, 1970;
Osborne & Byrnes, 1990;
Peterson, 1993.
121. Delisle, 1988;
Goertzel et al., 1978;
Lovecky, 1992;
Maker, 1982;
Osborne & Byrnes, 1990.
122. Osborne & Byrnes, 1990.
123. Osborne & Byrnes, 1990.
124. Cornell, 1992;
Hayes & Sloat, 1990;
Osborne & Byrnes, 1990.
125. Osborne & Byrnes, 1990;
Peterson, 1993.
126. Cornell, 1992;
Hayes & Sloat, 1990;
Osborne & Byrnes, 1990.
127. Hayes & Sloat, 1990;
Peterson, 1992;
128. Lovecky, 1992.
129. Lovecky, 1992;
Osborne & Byrnes, 1990;
Peterson, 1993.
130. Lovecky, 1992.
131. McGreevey, 1992.
132. Nielsen et al., 1993.
133. Nielsen et al., 1993.
134. McGreevey, 1992.
135. Nielsen et al., 1993.
136. McGreevey, 1992;
Nielsen et al., 1993.
137. McGreevey, 1992;
Nielsen et al., 1993.
138. McGreevey, 1992.
139. Nielsen et al., 1993.
140. Nielsen et al., 1993.
141. McGreevey, 1992.

Traits of Gifted Physically Disabled Students

Gifted physically disabled students have orthopedic handicaps (bone or muscle disorders) or health impairments (systemic diseases affecting more of the body). In some ways, these students display less complicated behavioral profiles than do high-potential students with mild handicaps. Unlike high-potential LD, ED, and communication-disordered pupils, gifted physically handicapped students are described in the literature almost completely with positive characteristics, as seen in Table 3.

This positive portrayal is in line with the generally positive attitude held by the public toward the physically disabled—an outlook that is positive, relative to other groups with disabilities.[1] Thus, this constructive portrayal of gifted physically disabled students has the potential to energize already positive-thinking parents, policy makers, teachers, and citizens to look more for giftedness among the physically disabled.

Learning

In particular contrast to the gifted learning disabled, high-potential physically handicapped students are described as excelling at both the higher and lower levels of learning. Some of them may demonstrate an impressive fund of factual knowledge,[2] in spite of learning time that has been missed due to their disabilities.[3] They may observe visual phenomena particularly well,[4] and learn and recall especially proficiently with their visual modalities.[5]

Even with limited mobility and fewer tangible learning experiences than many of their classmates, they are strong in learning abstract concepts.[6] Deductive reasoning and other analytical thinking skills[7] may help them to learn advanced concepts.

Gifted students with physical disabilities appear to learn particularly well through reading, which they may enjoy or do especially often.[8] Their emphasis on reading may be related in some cases to their some-times stationary status, which provides them more time for reading. They may display advanced oral-expressive vocabularies,[9] which are per-haps derived from their extensive reading or from the personal attention they receive from gregarious adults during illnesses.

In their overall academic development, these pupils' grades initially may dip due to lost school time or diminished energy.[10] Limited time or energy may lead to patterns of academic inconsistency.[11] When back in school after such absences, these students may close learning and achievement gaps relatively quickly.[12]

Motivation

In approaching learning tasks, high-potential pupils with physical disabilities desire challenges which are both broad and high. They demonstrate a desire for acquiring information in various subject areas, as well as information at higher intellectual levels.[13] They consistently put a remarkable amount of energy into learning those skills that they enjoy and in which they feel they will excel.[14]

Creativity

Gifted students with physical impairments often apply their creative energies toward solving personal problems, or they may direct their capabil-ities toward artistic expression. They may devise time-, space-, or energy-efficient solutions to their personal difficulties.[15] In their isolation, they also may concentrate effectively on producing creative music, writing, or art.[16]

Leadership/Social Development

The consistent pattern of strengths shown by high-potential physi-cally handicapped students in the areas of learning, motivation, and cre-ativity is not seen in social development. Admittedly, they enjoy exploring their environments,[17] demonstrating sensitivity toward peers in that environment,[18] and expressing concern for peers openly.[19] Yet they may suffer considerable isolation from those peers.[20] The stigma of their physical differences, to some extent, may drive peers away from them, which may lead to low self-esteem.[21] One physically disabled per-son expressed a common reaction to this stigma when he said, "I'm a person, not a wheelchair!"[22]

Additional Traits
of the Gifted Orthopedically Impaired

Like the traits of all high-potential physically disabled youth, the additional, distinctive traits of the gifted orthopedically handicapped are described in the literature as mostly positive.

Learning

As seen in Table 3, high-potential orthopedically impaired students share with gifted LD and ED pupils the ability to recall facts.[23] In fact, they may obtain average or above-average grades when healthy enough to be present in school.[24]

As revealed in Table 7, many of the gifted orthopedically impaired demonstrate their broad knowledge well through speaking and writing, even though this communication may be slowed by motoric limitations.[25] In performing daily living activities, as well as academic tasks, they may use compensatory strategies with particular effectiveness.[26]

Some of these pupils may display surprisingly adept perceptual-motor skills in personal mobility, both at home and in the neighborhood[27] (Table 7). However, they may have trouble in responding to, or even participating in, perceptual-motor activities in school, due to physical barriers in the learning environment.[28] Teachers would do well to allow extra time for some of these pupils to respond, because there often is a time-lag between their speedy reasoning and their slow (though eventually effective) expression of that thinking.[29]

Motivation

Not only is there a dichotomy between reasoning and performance in high-potential orthopedically impaired students, but there may be some dichotomies between their outwardly apparent and inwardly felt school motivations.

As seen in Table 3, these gifted students sometimes may quit difficult classroom tasks relatively early[30] due to a lack of energy or mobility. They may feel frustrated by their academic outcomes, which are not as good as they would like them to be.[31]

Despite frustrations, these pupils' overall scholastic outcomes nonetheless may turn out to be satisfactory, even with absences[32] (Table 7). However, these students, in their drive for normality,[33] may be disappointed with their results because of their high, self-set achievement standards.[34] Some of these pupils appear to believe that they will achieve "normality" only when they outstrip the "normal" person in achievement.[35]

In their efforts to achieve, gifted students with orthopedic impairments may appeal to classroom assistants for help, but they really need

Table 7

Additional Traits of the Gifted Orthopedically Impaired

Learning	Motivation	Creativity	Leadership
1. Effective speaking, writing [WM]	6. Satisfactory school work despite absences [Fg]	14. Liking for poetry [Fg]	17. Concern with own appearance [M82]
2. Adept use of compensatory techniques [WM]	7. Desire for normality [WM]	15. Innovativeness [WM]	18. Athleticism [WM]
3. Perceptual-motor strengths [Fg; WM]	8. High achievement standards [WM]	16. Search for school-policy changes [WM]	19. Concern with relationships [M82; WM]
4. Problems with physical barriers [WM]	9. Need for self-direction [Fg; M77; WM]		20. Good relationships with gifted [M77]
5. Reasoning-response lag [WM]	10. Outward equanimity [WM]		
	11. Inward stress, frustration [M82; WM]		
	12. Concern for future [WM]		
	13. Liking for outdoors [Fg]		

Fg   Fagerstrom, 1988
JC   Johnsen & Corn, 1989
M77 Maker, 1977
M82 Maker, 1982
WM Whitmore & Maker, 1985

self-direction more than they need outside assistance[36] (Table 7). They may show outer placidity in daily classroom situations,[37] while suffering from inner stress and frustration, particularly over their failures and uncertain futures.[38] They outwardly may accept being cooped up in a restrictive physical environment, even though they sometimes might hint that they really would prefer to move outdoors.[39]

Creativity

Humor, like scholastic performance, is a way in which high-potential pupils with orthopedic impairments seek outlets for their problems. These students may even make humorous jokes about their own handicaps[40] (Table 3).

They also may seek creative and contemplative escapes from their disabilities by reading poetry[41] (Table 7). In addition, they may show innovative, effective strategies for accomplishing visual tasks—strategies which will get around their disabilities.[42] In addition, they may advocate for changes in school policies, so that they may "be themselves" there, as fully functioning and comfortable persons with disabilities.[43]

Leadership/Social Development

Gifted orthopedically impaired pupils' creative schemes for "being themselves" may not always be effective or lead to popularity with their peers. However, there are two reasons for hope in assessing the potential future social development of this group. First, the problems of pupils with physical impairments may be understood better by their peers than the difficulties of other disabled students[44] (Table 3). Because of this greater understanding, peers may be more positive toward these students.

Second, high-potential students with orthopedic impairments themselves are often actively concerned with fitting in. They want to know if they have a pleasing physical appearance[45] and even wish to excel at athletics to the best of their abilities[46] (Table 7). Many also are concerned with maintaining good relationships with others,[47] and may develop particularly good relationships with gifted peers.[48]

Additional Traits
of the Gifted Health Impaired

The literature on the distinctive traits of high-potential health-impaired students is much sparser than readings specific to the gifted orthopedically impaired. The literature on gifted health-impaired students with cancer, asthma, allergies, and heart problems offers four additional traits beyond those attributed to the gifted physically handicapped in general. The characteristics that do appear are positive ones (like the additional traits of high-potential orthopedically impaired students), and sometimes are linked to their separation from other students.

Learning

While ill, many gifted students with health impairments spend time in unstructured (but educational) reading and listening activities that stimulate their language development (Table 3). These pupils embrace a "stimulating solitude" while recovering from their illnesses. Solitude allows these students time for the introspection sometimes necessary for higher level thinking[49] (Table 8).

They might take time out from this isolation to seek information about their own illnesses and treatments[50] (Table 8). And, when back in school, these reflective, analytical students may excel in mathematics, perhaps because background knowledge in math is consistent and can be made up with relative ease.[51]

Motivation

In their relative isolation, gifted students with health impairments benefit from the inspiring adults who visit them[52] (Table 8). Adults can tell interesting, exciting, or enlightening stories and can use advanced vocabulary. Both the story format and the vocabulary seem to spur learning in these students. One famous, inspiring adult was mentor/mother Rose Kennedy, who nurtured her bedridden son John with historical and political stories and lively banter.[53]

Creativity

Some high-potential health-impaired students may utilize their creativity and inspiration to devise their own methods for pain control, so they don't have to rely on drugs or others' often ineffective pain control measures[54] (Table 8).

Leadership

Gifted health-impaired students with leadership skills maintain those competencies when ill. They may continue wanting to spend time with their friends, to be popular with visitors, and to maintain control over many aspects of their treatment[55] (Table 8).

Table 8

Additional Traits of the Gifted Health Impaired

Learning	Motivation	Creativity	Leadership
1. Introspection [GGG]	4. Interaction with stimulating adults [GGG]	5. Self-devised methods for control of pain [SL]	6. Desires to be with friends [SL]
2. Seeks information about illness, treatment [SL]			7. Popular with visiting peers [SL]
3. Mathematically talented [WGO]			8. Chooses own course of action in treatment [SL]

GGG Goertzel, Goertzel, & Goertzel, 1978
SL Stephenson & Leroux, 1994
WGO Wiley & Goldstein, 1991

Notes

1. Rizzi, D. (1984). *Attitude change toward the physically handicapped through the use of film.* (Report NO. EC190945). (Doctoral dissertation, University of Sarasota, 1984). Ann Arbor, MI: University Microfilms International. (ERIC Document Reproduction Service No. ED 262537).
2. Goertzel et al., 1978.
3. Fagerstrom, E. M. G. (1988, May/June). The blossoming of Jeanie. *G/C/T, 11*(3), 23–24.
4. Fagerstrom, 1988.
5. Goertzel et al., 1978.
6. Goertzel et al., 1978;
   Whitmore & Maker, 1985.
7. Goertzel et al., 1978;
   Maker, 1982;
   Whitmore & Maker, 1985.
8. Fagerstrom, 1988;
   Goertzel et al., 1978.
9. Goertzel et al., 1978;
   Maker, 1982.
10. Fagerstrom, 1988.
11. Fagerstrom, 1988;
    Goertzel et al., 1978.
12. Goertzel et al., 1978;
    Whitmore & Maker, 1985.
13. Goertzel et al., 1978;
    Whitmore & Maker, 1985.
14. Goertzel et al., 1978.
15. Goertzel et al., 1978;
    Whitmore & Maker, 1985.
16. Fagerstrom, 1988;
    Goertzel et al., 1978.
17. Goertzel et al., 1978;
    Johnsen & Corn, 1989;
    Maker, 1977.
18. Goertzel et al., 1978.
19. Goertzel et al., 1978.
20. Goertzel et al., 1978.
21. Goertzel et al., 1978.
22. Winter, M., & DeSimone, D. (1983). I'm a person, not a wheelchair: Problems of disabled adolescents. In R. L. Jones (Ed.), *Reflections on growing up disabled* (pp. 27–33). Reston, VA: Council for Exceptional Children.
23. Whitmore & Maker, 1985.

24. Fagerstrom, 1988.
25. Whitmore & Maker, 1985.
26. Whitmore & Maker, 1985.
27. Fagerstrom, 1988;
    Whitmore & Maker, 1985.
28. Whitmore & Maker, 1985.
29. Whitmore & Maker, 1985.
30. Fagerstrom, 1988;
    Goertzel et al., 1978.
31. Fagerstrom, 1988;
    Whitmore & Maker, 1985.
32. Fagerstrom, 1988.
33. Whitmore & Maker, 1985.
34. Whitmore & Maker, 1985.
35. Whitmore & Maker, 1985.
36. Fagerstrom, 1988;
    Maker, 1977;
    Whitmore & Maker, 1985.
37. Whitmore & Maker, 1985.
38. Maker, 1982;
    Whitmore & Maker, 1985.
39. Fagerstrom, 1988.
40. Johnsen & Corn, 1989.
41. Fagerstrom, 1988.
42. Whitmore & Maker, 1985.
43. Whitmore & Maker, 1985.
44. Rizzi, 1984.
45. Maker, 1982.
46. Whitmore & Maker, 1985.
47. Maker, 1982;
    Whitmore & Maker, 1985.
48. Maker, 1977.
49. Goertzel et al., 1978.
50. Stephenson, D., & Leroux, J. A. (1994). Portrait of a creatively gifted child facing cancer. *Creativity Research Journal, 7*, 71–77.
51. Wiley, J., & Goldstein, D. (1991). Sex and allergy: Are they related to academic giftedness? *Journal for the Education of the Gifted, 14*, 412–422.
52. Goertzel et al., 1978.
53. Goertzel et al., 1978.
54. Stephenson & Leroux, 1994.
55. Stephenson & Leroux, 1994.

3

Traits of Gifted Sensory-Impaired Students

Compared to the gifted physically handicapped, high-potential sensory-impaired students display more relative strengths (as detailed in Table 3). In other words, the gifted physically impaired may shine relative to the general population in some skills, but the gifted sensory impaired sometimes stand out compared to nongifted hearing-impaired children and nongifted visually impaired youth.[1] The relativity of the gifts of the sensory impaired are especially apparent in this population's learning characteristics.

Learning

These pupils' ease in learning, compared to their non-hearing peers, often is related to the age of onset of their visual or hearing impairments. High-potential sensory-impaired children learn more easily when they acquire their impairments at a later age.[2]

This caveat aside, there appear to be several traits shown consistently by the gifted sensory impaired. They may demonstrate a good understanding of abstract concepts compared to other hearing and visually impaired students,[3] although they may have difficulty with these concepts compared to the general student population, particularly in the area of language.[4]

Despite some possible language-learning difficulties, high-potential sensory-impaired pupils seem to enjoy reading,[5] and often earn at least average grades in that subject.[6] They may be consistent in their grades across academic subjects during a given academic year.[7]

If academic deficits do exist in basic skills, these pupils may begin to close them as they grow older. Like Helen Keller, with age, they may "crack the code" of the mysterious processes of reading and writing.[8]

Motivation

Striving to succeed scholastically, like other high-potential children, the gifted sensory impaired may display great frustration when they fail to complete basic-skills tasks correctly.[9] In spite of this failure, these pupils seem highly motivated to master both basic skills and higher-level intellectual competencies.[10] They effectively channel their enormous energy into particular strengths and interests.[11]

Creativity

In the absence of seeing and hearing traditional ways of solving problems, the gifted sensory impaired may use some of their creative energy to devise highly imaginative solutions to their difficulties.[12] In addition, they may predict (considering their limited experience) what will happen in various situations, if various potential solutions are tried.[13]

High-potential students with sensory impairments also may make humorous comments, including remarks that center on their own disabilities.[14] When one gifted visually impaired student in my school was confronted by a well-meaning instructor who stood in front of the student's face and shouted questions, the pupil retorted, "I'm blind, not deaf!"

Leadership/Social Development

As part of their drive toward obtaining as normal treatment as possible in their social surroundings, high-potential sensory-impaired students enjoy actively exploring the people and places in their environments, despite the hazards posed by hard-to-hear or hard-to-see environmental obstacles.[15] Parents may allow or actively encourage such exploration in their gifted children with sensory impairments.[16] However, gifted students with visual or hearing impairments often may initiate explorations on their own.[17] As they explore their classroom environments and beyond, they appear to make a strong impression on others, but often negatively; observers tend to comment on what these students cannot do, rather than on what they can accomplish.[18]

Additional Traits of the Gifted Visually Impaired

The additional, distinctive traits of high-potential visually impaired pupils have been perceived as positive ones, just as the supplemental characteristics of the gifted orthopedically impaired and health impaired have been.

Learning

As displayed in Table 3, gifted students with visual impairments may recall facts,[19] as well as concepts that build on those facts.[20] In part, this talent for acquiring facts appears rooted in a highly accurate recall for things heard[21]—a memory that helps them compensate for their poor visual recall.[22]

Not surprisingly, because of their limited vision, these pupils tend to have problems in logically thinking through solutions to visually based dilemmas[23] (Table 3). However, those gifted visually impaired students with auditory strengths may display fine receptive and expressive vocabularies.[24]

While visual perception may be poor, social perceptiveness may be strong,[25] as seen in Table 9. High-potential visually impaired students may quickly grasp the general meaning of many lessons,[26] although they may more slowly understand the specific underlying principles of these lessons.[27] The use of efficient learning strategies, or "short cuts," helps these students reach an understanding of core concepts of reading and lectures, so they can achieve good grades.[28]

Motivation

Perhaps because of their slowness to grasp underlying principles and apply these principles to new tasks, the gifted visually impaired may not show interest or persistence in performing varying versions of rote classroom tasks[29] (Table 3). In addition, they may slowly perform other routine classroom activities[30] (Table 9).

They may enjoy learning considerably,[31] and may concentrate particularly well in, their strong academic subjects[32] (Table 9). They also may demonstrate special preference for concrete learning experiences,[33] activities with tools,[34] and independent expression of knowledge.[35]

Creativity

Based on their keen appreciation and memory for sounds, and their sensitivity to the differences between tones, high-potential visually impaired pupils may excel at music[36] (Table 3).

They also may demonstrate imaginativeness in their daily academic assignments,[37] providing multiple elaborations on a single written stimulus[38] (Table 9). In addition, they may adapt well to new academic situations and to new personal stresses.[39]

Leadership

Unlike many of the gifted hearing impaired, high-potential visually impaired students can quickly adapt to new auditory stimuli, and can

Table 9

Additional Traits of the Gifted Visually Impaired

Learning	Motivation	Creativity	Leadership
1. Perceptiveness [Jhn86]	4. Slow task performance [Jhn86]	10. Imaginativeness [Jhn86; WM]	14. Desire for normality [JC]
2. Quick understanding of most lessons [Jhn86]	5. Enjoyment of learning [Jhn86]	11. Elaborations on one stimulus [Jhn86]	15. Dominating personality [Scl]
3. Slow understanding of underlying principles [M82]	6. Concentration in strong areas [WM]	12. Adaptations in academics [WM]	16. Graceful physical movement [Psk]
4. Use of efficient learning strategies [ECW]	7. Desire for concrete learning [M77]	13. Skill in personal coping [WM]	
	8. Desire for tools [M77]		
	9. Desire for independent expression [Jhn86; M77]		

ECW	Erin, Corn, & Wolffle, 1993
JC	Johnsen & Corn, 1989
Jhn86	Johnson, 1986
M77	Maker, 1977
M82	Maker, 1982
Psk	Paskiewicz, 1986
Scl	Schale, 1972, cited in Maker, 1977
WM	Whitmore & Maker, 1985

effectively listen and speak with others.[40] Thus, they can more effectively express their concern for, and sensitivity to, their peers[41] (Table 3). Effective listening, speaking, and concern is appreciated by peers, and may account for the healthy self-esteem in many of the gifted visually impaired.[42] As described in Table 9, this concern appears to be part of an assertive drive toward "normality."[43] This drive may be marked in social settings by a dominating personality[44] and by graceful movement.[45]

Additional Traits of the Gifted Hearing Impaired

There are numerous traits of high-potential hearing-impaired students, some of which are considerably different from the supplementary characteristics of the gifted visually impaired.

Learning

As suggested by Table 3, because the gifted hearing impaired have understandable difficulties in listening, they perform poorly on auditorially based memory tasks.[46] However, perhaps in compensation for their listening problems, they do well on visual memory tasks.[47] Their performance is especially proficient in analyzing situations logically (based on their keen visual observations), though their logic is very "concrete" in nature.[48]

Some high-potential students with hearing impairments heretofore have been the beneficiary of culturally cohesive residential schools filled with other deaf and hard-of-hearing students[49] (Table 10). At such schools, these pupils often have been academically accelerated.[50] Some gifted hearing-impaired students at both residential and day schools have benefited academically from hearing aids.[51]

High-potential students with hearing impairments display varied academic[52] and perceptual-motor[53] interests. They make good decisions in diverse real-life situations.[54] They also express themselves well (verbally and nonverbally) in those situations, using lip-reading, gestures, and speech effectively.[55]

Motivation

Table 10 indicates that the gifted hearing impaired have diverse, positive, motivational traits, as well as various helpful expressive-language skills. They show great curiosity for many types of subject matter,[56] and sometimes take the initiative in pursuing their own education when their formal schooling falls short of the mark.[57]

Gifted hearing-impaired pupils desire to prove their own educational worth through their scholastic performances[58] (Table 10). They concentrate well on assigned tasks,[59] complete them in a well-organized fashion,[60] and become frustrated when the outcomes of these activities are not up to their expectations.[61] These students are likely to concentrate particularly well when taught with educational filmstrips.[62]

Creativity

Just as high-potential hearing-impaired students enjoy the creative informational input provided by filmstrips, so they also display divergent output effectively. In their work, they often exhibit imaginativeness[63] and accuracy in predictions[64] (Table 10).

Leadership/Social Development.

As shown in Table 3, gifted hearing-impaired pupils may be separated from their hearing peers by virtue of their disabilities,[65] despite the potential for creative excellence, and the positive peer recognition that could come from that creative production. Impairments increase the time and effort required for communication, by both high-potential hearing-impaired students and by their hearing classmates.[66] These time-consuming impairments discourage attempts at communication by fellow students. Because of their social isolation and academic underachievement, the gifted hearing impaired may display self-esteem problems.[67]

On the other hand, as seen in Table 10, these youngsters demonstrate a drive for "normality" and a place in the educational mainstream.[68] While they may exhibit self-consciousness and immaturity at times,[69] they nonetheless possess sufficient social skills to earn leadership roles, especially among their hearing-impaired peers.[70]

The leadership of the gifted hearing-impaired students may be marked by heavy involvement in school activities, which may involve the teaching of hearing students and the invitation of deaf adult speakers [71] to their schools. These leadership activities may help high-potential hearing-impaired pupils to compensate somewhat for the isolation they endure at both school and home[72] (Table 10).

Table 10

Additional Traits of the Gifted Hearing Impaired

Learning	Motivation	Creativity	Leadership
1. School is sensitive to hearing-impaired culture [VLL]	9. Curiosity about subject matter [M81; WM]	16. Imaginativeness [FMP]	18. Desire for normality, mainstream [M77; WM]
2. Academically accelerated [VLL]	10. Initiative-taking [WAW]	17. Good predictive abilities [WAW]	19. Self-consciousness [Lbm]
3. Hearing-aid benefits [CSG]	11. Desire to prove worth [WM]		20. Immaturity [Lbm]
4. Various academic interests [WM]	12. Task concentration [WM]		21. Leadership among hearing impaired peers [FMP]
5. Perceptual-motor interests, strengths [FMP; MBH; WM]	13. Good organization [FMP]		22. Extracurricular involvement at school [CSG]
6. Good decision-making [FMP]	14. Academic frustration [WM]		23. Seeking of deaf adults for school [CSG]
7. Language strengths: Non-verbal, symbolic, lip-reading [WAW; WM]	15. Liking of educational film-strips [Ldg]		24. Teaching hearing students about deaf culture [CSG]
8. Near-normal speech [WM]			25. Isolation at home [CSG]

CSG	Charlson, Strong, & Gold, 1993	M77 Maker, 1977
F	Farr, cited in Maker, 1977	M81 Maker, 1981
FMP	Fleury, MacNeil, & Pflaum 1981	M82 Maker, 1982
		VLL Vernon & LaFalce-Landers, 1994
Lbm	Lieberman, 1974, cited in Maker, 1977	WAW Whiting, Anderson, & Ward, 1981
Ldg	Lieding, 1981	WM Whitmore & Maker, 1985

Notes

1. Maker, 1982.
2. Fleury, P., MacNeil, B., & Pflaum, M. (1981). Media design for the gifted hearing impaired. *American Annals of the Deaf, 125*, 715–721;
   Goertzel et al., 1978;
   Whitmore & Maker, 1985.
3. Goertzel et al., 1978;
   Whiting, S. A., Anderson, L., & Ward, J. (1980). Identification of the mentally gifted minor deaf child in the public school system. *American Annals of the Deaf, 124*, 27–34;
   Whitmore & Maker, 1985.
4. Fleury et al., 1981;
   Goertzel et al., 1978;
   Whitmore & Maker, 1985.
5. Goertzel et al., 1978.
6. Lieding, R. (1981). Use of educational media in preparing gifted hearing-impaired children for early mainstreaming. *American Annals of the Deaf, 125*, 607–611;
   Whitmore & Maker, 1985.
7. Whiting et al., 1981.
8. Lieding, 1981;
   Whitmore & Maker, 1985.
9. Maker, 1982;
   Whitmore & Maker, 1985.
10. Goertzel et al., 1978.
11. Fleury et al., 1981;
    Goertzel et al., 1978;
    Paskiewicz, M. (1986). Mainstreaming the gifted visually impaired child. *Journal of Visual Impairment and Blindness, 80*, 973–988.
12. Fleury et al., 1981;
    Whiting et al., 1981;
    Whitmore & Maker, 1985.
13. Whiting et al, 1981.
14. Fleury et al., 1981;
    Johnsen & Corn, 1989.
15. Johnsen & Corn, 1989;
    Maker, 1977;
    Whitmore & Maker, 1985.
16. Whitmore & Maker, 1985.
17. Goertzel et al., 1978;
    Whitmore & Maker, 1985.
18. Johnsen & Corn, 1989;
    Whitmore & Maker, 1985.

19. Whitmore & Maker, 1985.
20. Goertzel et al., 1978.
21. Maker, 1982.
22. Whitmore & Maker, 1985.
23. Whitmore & Maker, 1985.
24. Goertzel et al., 1978;
    Maker, 1982.
25. Johnson, 1986.
26. Johnson, 1986.
27. Maker, 1982.
28. Erin, J. N., Corn, A. J., & Wolffle, K. (1993). Learning and study strategies of secondary school students with visual impairments. *Journal of Visual Impairment and Blindness, 87*, 263–267.
29. Goertzel et al., 1978.
30. Johnson, 1986.
31. Johnson, 1986.
32. Whitmore & Maker, 1985.
33. Maker, 1977.
34. Maker, 1977.
35. Johnson, 1986;
    Maker, 1977.
36. Goertzel et al., 1978.
37. Johnson, 1986;
    Whitmore & Maker, 1985.
38. Johnson, 1986.
39. Whitmore & Maker, 1985.
40. Goertzel et al., 1978.
41. Goertzel et al., 1978.
42. Beaty, L. A. (1994). Psychological factors and academic success of visually impaired college students. *RE: View, 26*(3), 131–139;
    Erin et al., 1993.
43. Johnsen & Corn, 1989.
44. Schale, F. C. (1972). Exploring the potential of the monocularly blind for faster reading. *Academic Therapy, 7*, 401–410;
    Hermanson & LaDew, 1958 in Maker, 1977.
45. Paskiewicz, 1987.
46. Maker, 1982.
47. Fleury et al., 1981;
    Goertzel et al., 1978.
48. Fleury et al., 1981;
    Whitmore & Maker, 1985.
49. Vernon, M., & LaFalce-Landers, E. (1994). A longitudinal study of intellectually gifted deaf and hard of hearing people. *American Annals of the Deaf, 138*, 427–434.
50. Vernon & LaFalce-Landers, 1994.

51. Charlson, E., Strong, M., & Gold, R. (1993). How successful deaf teenagers experience and cope with isolation. *American Annals of the Deaf, 137*, 261–270.
52. Whitmore & Maker, 1985.
53. Fleury et al., 1981;
    Murphy–Berman, V., Witters, L., & Harding, R. (1985). Effect of giftedness, sex, and bottle shape on hearing impaired adolescents' performance on the water line task. *Journal for the Education of the Gifted, 8*, 273–283;
    Whitmore & Maker, 1985.
54. Fleury et al., 1981.
55. Whiting et al., 1981;
    Whitmore & Maker, 1985.
56. Maker, C. J. (1981). The gifted hearing–impaired student. *American Annals of the Deaf, 125*, 631–645;
    Whitmore & Maker, 1985.
57. Whiting et al., 1981.
58. Whitmore & Maker, 1985.
59. Whitmore & Maker, 1985.
60. Fleury et al., 1981.
61. Johnsen & Corn, 1989.
62. Lieding, 1981.
63. Fleury et al., 1981.
64. Whiting et al., 1981.
65. Goertzel et al., 1978.
66. Goertzel et al., 1978;
    Maker, 1977.
67. Goertzel et al., 1978;
    Maker, 1977.
68. Maker, 1977;
    Whitmore & Maker, 1985.
69. Maker, 1977.
70. Fleury et al., 1981.
71. Charlson et al., 1993.
72. Charlson et al., 1993.

4

Traits of Gifted Students With Multiple Disabilities

Despite their powerful and inspirational strengths, the final two populations in our study—the gifted multi-handicapped (high-potential pupils with two or more disabilities) and the gifted mentally handicapped (high-potential students with low intelligence test scores and subpar adaptive behavior in daily life situations)—are noted in the literature mostly for their learning, motivational, and social problems.

Learning

Unlike the high-potential sensory impaired, gifted multi-handicapped pupils, in their learning profiles, are described mainly in terms of their weaknesses. Because of the limited capabilities of their input modes, they have acquired limited knowledge,[1] as seen in Table 3. Deficient modes may be either auditory[2] or visual.[3]

Language learning may be particularly difficult for some of these students,[4] further contributing to the low language-arts grades sometimes found in inconsistent academic profiles of high-potential multi-handicapped students[5] (Table 3). Deficiencies with input modes "learning gaps".[6]

On the positive side, when given information that they can process through efficiently operating input channels, these students can demonstrate rapid cognitive growth[7] (Table 11). Those with hearing and speech impairments may improve their oral-language skills quickly, when they finally "crack the linguistic code."[8] Gifted multi-handicapped students may be highly aware of their own uniqueness in learning oral-language and other skills.[9]

Table 11

Additional Traits of the Gifted Multiply Disabled

Learning	Motivation	Creativity	Leadership
1. Rapid cognitive growth [WM]	4. Skill, interest in setting goals [K54, 55]	6. Self-devised communication methods [Ksh]	7. Desire for normality [JC]
2. Oral language improvement [K54, 55]	5. Many intense frustrations [K54, 55; WM]		8. Limited mobility [WM]
3. Sense of own uniqueness [Ksh]			9. Temper [WM]

JC	Johnsen & Corn, 1989
K54	Keller, 1954, in Maker, 1977
K55	Keller, 1955, in Maker, 1977
Ksh	Kuschel, 1973, cited in Maker, 1977
WM	Whitmore & Maker, 1985

Motivation

Gifted multi-handicapped pupils' awareness of their unique potential, and their extreme difficulties in achieving that potential, may be responsible for their frustration over academic tasks[10] (Table 3). They nonetheless display tremendous persistence in attempting to fulfill their academic goals.[11]

Persistence in reaching ambitious, but realistic, goals may result in high achievement in deaf–blind populations[12] (Table 11). Frustrations over unachieved goals in academic or other realms may be particularly intense in gifted multi-handicapped students.[13]

Creativity

Despite the intensity of their frustrations, many of these students maintain a sense of humor[14] (Table 3). They also retain the energy to create effective ways of communicating with others[15] (Table 11).

Leadership/Social Development

Unfortunately, these pupils' communication competencies [16] do not attain for them integration with peers[17] (Table 3). Despite their desire for "normality,"[18] these students' sometimes large number of visually apparent differences from peers may set them too far apart, as may their limited mobility skills[19] and their tempers[20] (Table 11).

Notes

1. Goertzel et al., 1978.
2. Maker, 1982.
3. Goertzel et al., 1978.
4. Whitmore & Maker, 1985.
5. Goertzel et al., 1978.
6. Goertzel et al., 1978;
   Whitmore & Maker, 1985.
7. Whitmore & Maker, 1985.
8. Keller, H. (1954). *The story of my life*. Garden City, NY: Doubleday (cited in Maker, 1977); Keller, H. (1955). *Teacher*. Garden City, NY: Doubleday (cited in Maker, 1977).
9. Kuschel, R. (1973, October). The silent inventor: The creation of a sign language by the only mute on a Polynesian island. *Sign Language Studies*, 1–27 (cited in Maker, 1977).
10. Maker, 1982.
11. Goertzel et al., 1978.
12. Keller, 1954, 1955, cited in Maker, 1977.
13. Keller, 1954, 1955, cited in Maker, 1977;
    Whitmore & Maker, 1985.
14. Whitmore & Maker, 1985.
15. Kuschel, 1973, cited in Maker, 1977.
16. Johnson & Corn, 1989.
17. Goertzel et al., 1978.
18. Johnsen & Corn, 1989.
19. Whitmore & Maker, 1985.
20. Whitmore & Maker, 1985.

Traits of Gifted Mentally Handicapped Students

The 1977–1989 literature on gifted persons with mental disabilities is limited to two case studies.[1] Perhaps even more than the gifted multi-handicapped, high-potential mentally handicapped students are characterized in these two articles by what they cannot do, rather than what they can do. This focus on the negative is particularly pronounced in the area of learning traits.

Learning

As suggested by Table 3, gifted students with mental disabilities seem to have a fund of knowledge that is limited to one special area.[2] They have acquiring and remembering facts.[3] This is due to auditory recall difficulties[4] and visual memory problems.[5] They also have trouble with higher-level intellectual skills, specifically analytical thinking,[6] the understanding of language concepts,[7] and the comprehension of other abstract generalizations.[8]

Scholastically, these students generally are poor in reading skills,[9] and obtain overall low grades[10] (Table 3). Writing competencies may be particularly poor,[11] although speech skills may improve over time[12] (Table 12).

Motivation

Not surprisingly, due to skill problems at lower and higher levels, high-potential pupils with mental impairments may be extremely frustrated over academic tasks[13] (Table 3). While they are persistent in their strong areas,[14] these students have a narrow attention span in many other areas[15] (Table 12).

Table 12

Additional Traits of the Gifted Mentally Handicapped

Learning	Creativity
1. Poor writing [NK]	4. Strengths in painting, music [Msh; NK]
2. Gradual speech improvement [NK]	5. Feelings communicated through artwork [NK]

Motivation	
3. Narrow attention span [Msh]	

Msh	Morishima, 1974
NK	Newcomb & Kilbourn, 1973

Creativity

As indicated in Table 12, attention spans may be impressive in gifted mentally handicapped students' strengths, which tend to be painting or music.[16] These pupils may undertake such activities to communicate their feelings, and to exercise their creative skills.[17]

An Update

A recent review of the literature, and a follow-up set of case studies on gifted mentally handicapped persons, by Miller (1989) has greatly extended our profile of the learning, motivational, and creative traits of this population. From his book (not covered in Table 12, which includes just the types of readings covered by the rest of this monograph, namely journal articles and books on more than one gifted-disabled population), Miller noted that these students' learning profiles are characterized by delayed language development[18] and echolalia (the parrot-like repetition of others' words).[19] However, they display better academically related skill achievement than their mentally disabled peers,[20] and sometimes excel in the specific skill of calendar calculating.[21]

In motivational traits, high-potential mentally challenged students may be described by school personnel as being severely disturbed,[22] being autistic,[23] or having behavior problems.[24] Miller (1989), however, found in several of his own case studies that teachers may overreact to existing behavioral difficulties—obsessive behavior;[25] extreme hyperactivity, restlessness and unmanageable behavior;[26] and lethargy and withdrawal.[27]

In spite of behavioral difficulties, Miller's case studies were filled with tales of creativity. One case study included 16 contemporary, creative, musically adept savants who shared perfect pitch and easy recall for new melodies. Each of these persons played an instrument or listened extensively to the radio. Miller believed that these subjects could generalize their musical aptitude from one situation to another. He also held that instrument-playing subjects enjoyed better social adjustment than subjects who only listened to the radio.

Notes

1. Morishima, A. (1974). Another Van Gogh of Japan: The superior artwork of a retarded boy. *Exceptional Children, 41,* 92–96 (cited in Maker, 1977);
   Newcomb, D., & Kilbourn, M. (1973). An Andre exhibit. *Dialogue, 6,* 1, 5–6 (cited in Maker, 1977).
2. Morishima, 1974.
3. Newcomb & Kilbourn, 1973.
4. Morishima, 1974.
5. Newcomb & Kilbourn, 1973.
6. Newcomb & Kilbourn, 1973.
7. Morishima, 1974.
8. Morishima, 1974;
   Newcomb & Kilbourn, 1973.
9. Morishima, 1974.
10. Newcomb & Kilbourn, 1973.
11. Newcomb & Kilbourn, 1973.
12. Newcomb & Kilbourn, 1973.
13. Morishima, 1974.
14. Newcomb & Kilbourn, 1973.
15. Morishima, 1974.
16. Morishima, 1974;
    Newcomb & Kilbourn, 1973.
17. Newcomb & Kilbourn, 1973.
18. Goodman, J. (1972). A case study of an "autistic-savant." Mental function in the psychotic child with markedly discrepant abilities. *Journal of Child Psychology and Psychiatry, 13,* 267–278.
19. Anastasi, A., & Levee, R. F. (1960). Intellectual defect and musical talent: A case report. *American Journal of Mental Deficiency, 64,* 695–703.
20. Nichira, K., Foster, R., Shelhaas, M., & Leland, H. (1974). *Adaptive behavior scales: Manual.* Washington, DC: American Association of Mental Deficiency.
21. Goodman, 1972.
22. Duckett, J. (1977). Adaptive and maladaptive behavior of idiot savants. *American Journal of Mental Deficiency, 82,* 308–311.
23. Rimland, B. (1978). Inside the mind of the autistic savant. *Psychology Today, 12*(3), 69–80.
24. Duckett, 1977.
25. Lewis, M. (1985). Gifted or dysfunctional: The child savant. *Pediatric Annals, 14,* 733–742.
26. Critchley, D. L. (1979). The adverse influence of psychiatric labels on the obsessions of child behavior. *American Journal of Orthopsychiatry, 49,* 157–160.
27. Anastasi & Levee, 1960.

Conclusion

I t is important to close with a cautionary note about the appropriate uses of the presented traits, and with an indication of future directions needed in the study of gifted-disabled groups' characteristics.

Limitations on Uses of Trait Descriptions

The presented traits of twice-exceptional groups have limited use. Many of these characteristics lack research validation as distinctive traits of high-potential disabled students; thus, they should be employed by teachers, parents, legislators, and the public just as sets of *possible* indicators of giftedness in disabled populations.

Teachers will be tempted to regard these characteristics as surefire indicators, ones which will guarantee for their student possessors an educational label of gifted. Instead, educators should use these traits simply as one piece of evidence for making referrals, supplementing them with other, already-validated evidence that has shown potential for identifying giftedness in the disabled: nominations from peers,[1] from parents,[2] and from high-potential disabled students themselves.[3]

Parents, too, may become overly excited by the preceding trait lists. They may look for traits of giftedness for which they have never looked before, and see these characteristics where they truly don't exist in any pervasive way, in the hopes of seeing "official" giftedness in their children with disabilities. Parents should carefully read the text as well as the trait lists, in order to see how these traits may actually play themselves out in school. They can then report, in detail, their children's strengths to school officials, so that these personnel can help develop those strengths, even if those students are never placed in gifted programs.

Policymakers who read the trait descriptions and the lists should be applauded for their dedication; on the other hand, they may be tempted, from the collected body of literature, to think that the problem of identifying high-potential disabled students is well on the road to being solved. Questions about the validity of these checklists aside, the identification problem will remain a complicated one. This is because it still is not certain to what extent: (1) the trait descriptions will be used by teachers in their referrals of potentially gifted students, and (2) the descriptions will carry actual weight in schools' gifted education assessment processes.

Policymakers should think about the trait checklists as evidence that research has produced proof of the existence of the twice-exceptional. They should be moved to support more such research, to turn the accumulated literature on the traits of the gifted disabled into validated identification measures.

The public, perhaps even more than parents or legislators, may be tempted to look merely at lists of traits rather than at how those characteristics play themselves out. As a result, the public may see giftedness everywhere in disabled populations, encouraging many of the handicapped to seek the gifted label. They should appreciate the accomplishments of persons with disabilities whom they know, and encourage these persons to seek additional, stimulating experiences in their areas of expertise.

Needs for Further Investigation on Traits

The public, like parents, educators, and policymakers, inevitably will play roles in determining the actual uses of the presented trait lists in efforts to identify the twice-exceptional. But, it is one particular group of educators—educational researchers—who hold the key to determining the composition of the lists. It is these researchers who will find more valid and reliable indicators than are contained in these current lists. It is they who will movingly write about distinctive gifted-disabled characteristics so that people will visualize these traits and want to find them. And, it is they who will arrange these traits in understandable, time-efficient, observational instruments that can be utilized in community, general-education, high-potential, and special-education settings.

It is perhaps they who will be most challenged by this monograph.

Notes

1. Davis & Rimm, 1985.
2. Davis & Rimm, 1985.
3. Eisenberg, D., & Epstein, E., 1981.

References

Aaron, P. G., Phillips, S., & Larsen, S. (1988). Specific reading disability in historically famous persons. *Journal of Learning Disabilities, 21,* 523–538.

Abroms, K. (1978). Gifted and learning disabled. *G/C/T, 1*(2), 26–28.

Anastasi, A., & Levee, R. F. (1960). Intellectual defect and musical talent: A case report. *American Journal of Mental Deficiency, 64,* 695–703.

Baker, H. J. (1970). *Biographical sagas of willpower.* New York: Vantage Press.

Baldwin, L. J., & Garguilo, D. A. (1983). A model program for elementary-age learning-disabled/gifted children. In L. H. Fox, L. Brody, & D. Tobin (Eds.), *Learning-disabled/gifted children: Identification and programming* (pp. 207–222). Baltimore: University Park Press.

Barton, J. E., & Starnes, W. T. (1989). Identifying distinguishing characteristics of gifted and talented/learning disabled students. *Roeper Review, 12,* 23–29.

Baum, S. (1988). An enrichment program for gifted learning disabled students. *Gifted Child Quarterly, 32,* 226–230.

Baum, S., & Owen, S. V. (1988). High ability/learning disabled students: How are they different? *Gifted Child Quarterly, 32,* 311–316.

Beaty, L. A. (1994). Psychological factors and academic success of visually impaired college students. *Re: View, 26*(3), 131–139.

Bireley, M. M., Williamson, T., & Languis, M. (1992). Physiological uniqueness: A new perspective on the learning disabled/gifted child. *Roeper Review, 15,* 101–107.

Bow, J. N. (1988). A comparison of intellectually superior male reading achievers and underachievers from a neuropsychological perspective. *Journal of Learning Disabilities, 21,* 118–123.

Bricklin, P. M. (1983). Working with parents of learning-disabled/gifted children. In L. H. Fox, L. Brody, & D. Tobin (Eds.), *Learning-disabled/gifted children: Identification and programming* (pp. 243–260). Baltimore: University Park Press.

Brooks, P. (1972). *Bright delinquents: The story of a unique school.* London: The National Foundation for Educational Research in England & Wales.

Caplan, N. S., & Powell, M. A. (1964). A comparison of average to superior IQ delinquents. *Journal of Psychology, 54,* 307–318.

Charlson, E., Strong, M., & Gold, R. (1993). How successful deaf teenagers experience and cope with isolation. *American Annals of the Deaf, 137,* 261–270.

Chubb, J. E., & Moe, T. M. (1990). *Politics, markets, and America's schools.* Washington, DC: Brookings Institution.

Ciha, T. E. (1974). Parents as identifiers of giftedness: Ignored but accurate. *Gifted Child Quarterly, 18*, 191–195.

Coleman, M. R. (1992). A comparison of how gifted/LD and average/LD boys cope with school frustration. *Journal for the Education of the Gifted, 15*, 239–265.

Cornell, D. G. (1992). High intelligence and severe delinquency: Evidence disputing the connection. *Roeper Review, 14*, 233–239.

Critchley, D. L. (1979). The adverse influence of psychiatric labels on the obsessions of child behavior. *American Journal of Orthopsychiatry, 49*, 157–160.

Daniels, P. (1983). Teaching the learning-disabled/gifted child. In L. W. Fox, L. Brody, & D. Tobin (Eds.), *Learning-disabled/gifted children: Identification and programming* (pp. 37–49). Baltimore: University Park Press.

Das, J. P., Mishra, R. K., & Kirby, J. R. (1994). Cognitive patterns of children with dyslexia: A comparison between groups with high and average non-verbal intelligence. *Journal of Learning Disabilities, 27*, 235–242.

Dauber, S. L., & Benbow, C. P. (1990). Aspects of personality and peer relations of extremely talented adolescents. *Gifted Child Quarterly, 34*, 10–15.

Davis, G. A., & Rimm, S. B. (1985). *Education of the gifted and talented.* Englewood Cliffs, NY: Prentice-Hall.

Delisle, J. (1988, January/February). Striking out: Suicide and the gifted adolescent. *Gifted Child Today, 11*(1), 41–44.

Delisle, J. (1990). The gifted adolescent at risk: Strategies and resources for suicide prevention. *Journal for the Education of the Gifted, 13*, 212–228.

Denckla, M. (1988). Cited in "Myelin deposits affect brain activity, higher-level thinking." *TAG Update, 11*(3), 1.

Duckett, J. (1977). Adaptive and maladaptive behavior of idiot savants. *American Journal of Mental Deficiency, 82*, 308–311.

Eisenberg, D., & Epstein, E. (1981, December). *The discovery and development of giftedness in handicapped children.* Paper presented at the CEC-TAG Topical Conference on the Gifted and Talented Child, Orlando, FL.

Ellston, T. (1993, January/February). Gifted and learning-disabled ... A paradox? *Gifted Child Today, 16*(1), 17–19.

Erin, J. N., Corn, A. J., & Wolffle, K. (1993). Learning and study strategies of secondary school students with visual impairments. *Journal of Visual Impairment and Blindness, 87*, 263–267.

Fagerstrom, E. M. G. (1988, May/June). The blossoming of Jeanie. *Gifted Child Today, 11*(5), 23–24.

Fall, J., & Nolan, L. (1993, January/February). A paradox of exceptionalities. *Gifted Child Today, 16*(1), 46–49.

Fleury, P., MacNeil, B., & Pflaum, M. (1981). Media design for the gifted hearing impaired. *American Annals of the Deaf, 125*, 715–721;

Fox, L. H. (1981). Identification of the academically gifted. *American Psychologist, 36*, 1103–1111.

Fox, L. H., Brody, L., & Tobin, D. (1983). *Learning-disabled/gifted children: Identification and programming*. Baltimore: University Park Press.

Friedrichs, T. P. (1990). *Gifted handicapped students: The way forward*. Richmond, VA: Virginia Department of Education.

Gallagher, P. A. (1966). *An art media procedure for developing creativity in emotionally disturbed children*. Unpublished master's thesis, University of Kansas, Lawrence.

Gallagher, P. A. (1972). Procedures for developing creativity in emotionally disturbed children. *Focus on Exceptional Children, 4*, 1–9.

Gath, D., Tenneth, G., & Pidduck, R. (1970). Educational characteristics of bright delinquents. *British Journal of Educational Psychology, 40*, 216–219.

Gerber, P. J., Ginsberg, R., & Reiff, H. B. (1992). Identifying alterable patterns in employment success for highly successful adults with learning disabilities. *Journal of Learning Disabilities, 25*, 475–487.

Goertzel, M. G., Goertzel, V., & Goertzel, T. (1978). *300 eminent personalities*. San Francisco: Jossey-Bass.

Goodman, J. (1972). A case study of an "autistic-savant." Mental function in the psychotic child with markedly discrepant abilities. *Journal of Child Psychology and Psychiatry, 13*, 267–278.

Hallahan, D. P., & Kauffman, J. M. (1986). *Introduction to special education* (3rd ed.). Englewood Cliffs, NJ: Prentice-Hall.

Hannah, C. L., & Shore, B. M. (1995). Metacognition and high intellectual ability: Insights from the study of learning-disabled gifted students. *Gifted Child Quarterly, 39*, 95–109.

Harrington, R. G. (1982). Caution: Standardized testing may be hazardous to the health of intellectually gifted children. *Education, 103*, 112–117.

Harvey, S., & Seeley, K. R. (1984). An investigation of the relationships among intellectual and creative abilities, extracurricular activities, achievement and giftedness in a delinquent population. *Gifted Child Quarterly, 28*, 73–79.

Hayes, G. W. (1984). Unlocking the dyslexic teenage reader: Paul's gift. *Annals of Dyslexia, 28*, 186–193.

Hayes, M. L., & Sloat, R. S. (1990). Suicide and the gifted adolescent. *Journal for the Education of the Gifted, 13*, 239–244.

Hermanson, D., & LaDew, H. (1958). Some psychological and psychiatric findings on gifted students in San Diego. Unpublished manuscript cited in C. J. Maker (1977), *Providing programs for the gifted handicapped* (Reston, VA: Council for Exceptional Children).

Hollingworth, L. S. (1942). *Children with above 180 IQ*. Yonkers-on-Hudson, NY: World Book.

Jansky, J. J. (1980). Language disability: A case study. *Annals of Dyslexia, 30*, 252–267.

Johnsen, S. K., & Corn, A. L. (1989). The past, present, and future of education for gifted children with sensory and/or physical disabilities. *Roeper Review, 12*, 13–23.

Johnson, D. E. (1970). Personality characteristics in relation to college persistence. *Journal of Counseling Psychology, 17*, 162–167.

Johnson, L. (1987). Comment: Teaching the visually impaired gifted youngster. *Journal of Visual Impairment and Blindness, 81,* 51–52.

Jones, B. (1986). The gifted dyslexic. *Annals of Dyslexia, 36*, 301–317.

Keller, H. (1954). *The story of my life*. Garden City, NY: Doubleday (cited in Maker, 1977).

Keller, H. (1955). *Teacher*. Garden City, NY: Doubleday (cited in Maker, 1977).

Kolko, D. J., Ayllon, T., & Torrence, C. (1987). Positive practice routines in overcoming resistance to the treatment of school phobia: A case study with follow-up. *Journal of Behavior Therapy and Experimental Psychiatry, 18*, 249–253.

Kuschel, R. (1973, October). The silent inventor: The creation of a sign language by the only mute on a Polynesian island. *Sign Language Studies,* 1–27 (cited in Maker, 1977).

Levey, S., & Dolan, J. (1988, May/June). Addressing specific learning abilities in gifted students. *Gifted Child Today, 11*(3), 10–11.

Lewis, M. (1985). Gifted or dysfunctional: The child savant. *Pediatric Annals, 14*, 733–742.

Lieding, R. (1981). Use of educational media in preparing gifted hearing-impaired children for early mainstreaming. *American Annals of the Deaf, 125*, 607–611.

Lovecky, D. V. (1992). Exploring social and emotional aspects of giftedness in children. *Roeper Review, 15*, 18–25.

Mahoney, A. R. (1980). Gifted delinquents: What do we know about them? *Child and Youth Services Review, 2*, 315–330.

Maker, C. J. (1977). *Providing programs for the gifted handicapped*. Reston, VA: Council for Exceptional Children.

Maker, C. J. (1981). The gifted hearing-impaired student. *American Annals of the Deaf, 125*, 631–645.

Maker, C. J. (1982). *Curriculum development for the gifted*. Rockville, MD: Aspen.

Mautner, T. S. (1984). Dyslexia—my "invisible handicap." *Bulletin of the Orton Society, 34*, 299–311.

McCants, G. (1985, May/June). Suicide and the gifted. *G/C/T, 8*(3), 27–29.

McGreevey, A. (1992). All in the golden afternoon: The early life of Charles L. Dodgson (Lewis Carroll). *Gifted Child Quarterly, 36,* 6–10.

Miller, L. K. (1989). *Musical savants: Exceptional skill in the mentally retarded.* Hillsdale, NJ: Lawrence Erlbaum.

Mindell, P. (1982). The gifted dyslexic: A case study with theoretical and educational implications. *Roeper Review, 4,* 22–23.

Miner, M., & Siegel, L.S. (1992). William Butler Yeats: Dyslexic? *Journal of Learning Disabilities, 25,* 372–375.

Morishima, A. (1974). Another Van Gogh of Japan: The superior art-work of a retarded boy. *Exceptional Children, 41,* 92–96 (cited in Maker, 1977).

Murphy-Berman, V., Witters, L., & Harding, R. (1985). Effect of gift-edness, sex, and bottle shape on hearing impaired adolescents' performance on the water line task. *Journal for the Education of the Gifted, 8,* 273–283.

National Association for Gifted Children (NAGC). (1995). *Annual national convention program.* Washington, DC: Author.

National Association for Gifted Children (NAGC). (1999). *Annual national convention program.* Washington, DC: Author.

Newcomb, D., & Kilbourn, M. (1973). An Andre exhibit. *Dialogue, 6,* 1, 5–6 (cited in Maker, 1977).

Nichira, K., Foster, R., Shelhaas, M., & Leland, H. (1974). *Adaptive behavior scales: Manual.* Washington, DC: American Association of Mental Deficiency.

Nielsen, M. E., Higgins, L. D., Hammond, A. E., & Williams, R. A. (1993, September/October). Gifted children with disabilities. *Gifted Child Today, 16*(5), 9–12.

Odden, A., & Clune, W. (1995). Improving educational productivity and finance. *Educational Researcher, 24*(9), 6–10.

Osborne, J. K., & Byrnes, D. A. (1990, May/June). Gifted, disaffected, disruptive youth and the alternative school. *Gifted Child Today, 13*(3), 45–48.

Parker, H. K. (1970). On making incorrigible youths corrigible. *Journal of Secondary Education, 45,* 57–60.

Paskiewicz, M. (1986). Mainstreaming the gifted visually impaired child. *Journal of Visual Impairment and Blindness, 80,* 973–988.

Patten, M. B. (1972). Visually mediated thinking: A report on the case of Albert Einstein. *Journal of Learning Disabilities, 6,* 415–420.

Peterson, J. (1993, January/February). What we learned from Jenna. *Gifted Child Today, 16*(1), 15–16.

Pollack, C., & Branden, A. (1982). Odyssey of a "mirrored" personal-ity. *Annals of Dyslexia, 32,* 275–288.

Porter, R. M. (1982). The gifted handicapped: A status report. *Roeper Review, 4,* 24–25.

Rack, L. (1981). Developmental dyslexia and literary creativity: Creativity in the area of deficit. *Journal of Learning Disabilities, 14*, 262–263.

Rawson, M. (1968). *Developmental language disability: Adult accomplishments of dyslexic boys.* Baltimore: Johns Hopkins Press.

Renzulli, J. S., Hartman, R. K., & Callahan, C. M. (1971). Teacher identification of superior students. *Exceptional Children, 38*, 211–214.

Rimland, B. (1978). Inside the mind of the autistic savant. *Psychology Today, 12*(3), 69–80.

Rizzi, D. (1984). *Attitude change toward the physically handicapped through the use of film.* (Report No. EC190945). (Doctoral dissertation, University of Sarasota, 1984). Ann Arbor, MI: University Microfilms International. (ERIC Document Reproduction Service No. ED 262537)

Rosner, S. L., & Seymour, J. (1983). The gifted child with a learning disability: Clinical evidence. In L. H. Fox, L. Brody, & D. Tobin (Eds.), *Learning-disabled/gifted children: Identification and programming* (pp. 77–97). Baltimore: University Park Press.

Ryckman, D. B., & Elrod, E. F. (1984). Once is not enough. *Journal of Learning Disabilities, 16*, 87–89.

Sarnekcy, E., & Michaud, T. (1979). Local programs for gifted and talented hearing impaired students. *Language, Speech, and Hearing Services in the Schools, 10,* 191–194.

Savage, L., & Woodrum, D. (1988, May 6). *Presentation on identification of gifted LD students using Renzulli-Hartman Scales.* West Virginia TAG-GLD Conference, South Charleston, WV.

Schale, F. C. (1972). Exploring the potential of the monocularly blind for faster reading. *Academic Therapy, 7*, 401–410.

Schiff, M. M., Kaufman, A. S., & Kaufman, N. L. (1981). Scatter analysis of WISC-R profiles for learning disabled children with superior intelligence. *Journal of Learning Disabilities, 14*, 400–404.

Seeley, K.R. (1984). Perspectives on adolescent giftedness and delinquency. *Journal for the Education of the Gifted, 8*, 59–72.

Senf, G. M. (1983). The nature and identification of learning disabilities and their relationship to the gifted child. In L. H. Fox, L. Brody, & D. Tobin (Eds.), *Learning disabled/gifted children: Identification and programming.* Baltimore: University Park Press.

Steeves, K. J. (1983). Memory as a factor in the computational efficiency of dyslexic children with high abstract reasoning ability. *Annals of Dyslexia, 33*, 141–152.

Stephenson, D., & Leroux, J. A. (1994). Portrait of a creatively gifted child facing cancer. *Creativity Research Journal, 7*, 71–77.

Tannenbaum, A. J., & Baldwin, L. J. (1983). Giftedness and learning disability: A paradoxical combination. In L. H. Fox, L. Brody, & D. Tobin (Eds.), *Learning-disabled/gifted children: Identification and programming* (pp. 11–36). Baltimore: University Park Press.

Thompson, L. J. (1971). Language disabilities in men of eminence. *Journal of Learning Disabilities, 4,* 39–50.

Toll, M. F. (1993, January/February). Gifted learning–disabled: A kaleidoscope of needs. *Gifted Child Today, 16*(1), 34–35.

Udall, A. (1985). Chapter reaction. In J. R. Whitmore & C. J. Maker, *Intellectual giftedness in disabled persons* (pp. 207–209). Rockville, MD: Aspen.

Udall, A. J., & Maker, C. J. (1983). A pilot program for elementary-age learning–disabled gifted students. In L. H. Fox, L. Brody, & D. Tobin (Eds.), *Learning-disabled/gifted children: Identification and programming* (pp. 223–242). Baltimore: University Park Press.

U.S. Department of Education. (1987). *What works: Research about teaching and learning* (2nd ed.). Washington, DC: Office of Educational Research and Improvement.

VanTassel-Baska, J. (1991). Serving the disabled gifted through educational collaboration. *Journal for the Education of the Gifted, 14,* 246–266.

Vernon, M., & LaFalce-Landers, E. (1994). A longitudinal study of intellectually gifted deaf and hard of hearing people. *American Annals of the Deaf, 138,* 427–434.

Vespi, L., & Yewchuk, C. (1992). A phenomenological study of the social/emotional characteristics of gifted learning disabled children. *Journal for the Education of the Gifted, 16,* 55–72.

Waldron, K. A., & Saphire, D. G. (1990). An analysis of WISC-R factors for gifted students with learning disabilities. *Journal of Learning Disabilities, 23,* 491–498.

Wang, M. C., Reynolds, M. C., & Walberg, H. J. (1986). Rethinking special education. *Educational Leadership, 44*(1), 26–31.

Weaver, P. A., & Dickinson, D. K. (1979). Story comprehension and recall in dyslexic students. *Bulletin of the Orton Society,* 157–171.

Whiting, S. A., Anderson, L., & Ward, J. (1980). Identification of the mentally gifted minor deaf child in the public school system. *American Annals of the Deaf, 124,* 27–34.

Whitmore, J. R. (1980). *Giftedness, conflict, and underachievement.* Boston: Allyn and Bacon.

Whitmore, J. R. (1981). Gifted children with handicapping conditions: A new frontier. *Exceptional Children, 48,* 106–114.

Whitmore, J. R., & Maker, C. J. (1985). *Intellectual giftedness in disabled persons.* Rockville, MD: Aspen.

Whitmore, J. R., & Maker, C. J., & Knott, G. (1985). Intellectually gifted persons with specific learning disabilities. In J. R. Whitmore & C. J. Maker, *Intellectual giftedness in disabled persons* (pp. 175–206). Rockville, MD: Aspen.

Wiley, J., & Goldstein, D. (1991). Sex and allergy: Are they related to academic giftedness? *Journal for the Education of the Gifted, 14,* 412–422.

Will, M. (1986). *Educating children with learning problems: A shared responsibility*. Washington, DC: U.S. Department of Education, Office of Special Education.

Williams, K. (1988). The learning disabled gifted: An unmet challenge. *Gifted Child Quarterly, 11*, 17–18.

Wingenbach, N. (1985). Chapter reaction (to "Intellectually gifted persons with specific learning disabilities"). In J. R. Whitmore & C. J. Maker (Eds.), *Intellectual giftedness in disabled persons* (pp. 210–211). Rockville, MD: Aspen.

Winter, M., & DeSimone, D. (1983). I'm a person, not a wheelchair: Problems of disabled adolescents. In R. L. Jones (Ed.), *Reflections on growing up disabled* (pp. 27–33). Reston, VA: Council for Exceptional Children.

Ysseldyke, J., Algozzine, B., & Thurlow, M. (1992). *Critical issues in special education* (2nd ed.). Boston: Houghton-Mifflin.

•••

Appendix

Sources Consulted

Gifted Journals, 1979–1994

- *Creativity Research Journal* (1990–1994)
- *Gifted Child Quarterly*
- *Gifted Child Today* (formerly *Gifted/Creative/Talented*)
- *Journal for the Education of the Gifted*
- *Journal of Creative Behavior*
- *Roeper Review*

Books on Gifted Handicapped, 1977–1994

- Goertzel, M., Goertzel, V., & Goertzel, T. (1978)
- Maker, C.J. (1977)
- Maker, C.J. (1982)
- Whitmore, J.R., & Maker, C.J. (1985)

Handicapping—Area Journals, 1979–1994

Learning Disabilities
- *Annals of Dyslexia* (previously named *Bulletin of the Orton Society*)
- *Journal of Learning Disabilities*
- *Learning Disabilities Quarterly*
- *Learning Disabilities Research & Practice* (1985–1994)

Emotional Disturbance/Behavior Disorders
- *Behavioral Disorders*
- *Behavior Modification*
- *Journal of Behavior Therapy and Experimental Child Psychiatry*

Speech-Language Impairments
- *Hearing, Speech, and Language Services in the Schools*
- *Journal of Hearing and Speech Disorders*
- *Journal of Hearing and Speech Research*

Orthopedic Impairments
- No specific educational journals in this area.

Health Impairments
- *Health Education Quarterly*
- *Health Education Reports*
- *Journal of School Health*

Visual Impairments
- *Journal of Visual Impairment and Blindness*
- *RE: View* (formerly *Education of the Visually Handicapped*)

Hearing Impairments
- *American Annals of the Deaf*
- *Volta Review*

Multiple Handicaps
- No specific educational journals in this area.

Mental Retardation
- *American Journal of Mental Retardation* (formerly *American Journal of Mental Deficiency*)
- *Mental Retardation*
- *Education and Training of the Mentally Retarded*